Aromatic Gifts

in Classic Knitted Cotton

A display of lace knitting to be found in this book: crazy patchwork pillow *(instructions page 45)*, ellan mesh lace Cushion *(instructions page 32)*, patrician lace pillow *(instructions page 29)*, the doll is wearing a knitted lace trimmed dress featured in the book *Traditional Lace Knitting*.

Aromatic Gifts

in Classic Knitted Cotton

FURZE HEWITT

Dedicated to my grandchildren and their parents

ACKNOWLEDGMENTS

This book would not have been possible without the expertise and generous assistance of the following people:

Robert Roach, photographer, for his skill in photographing white lace knitting.

Josephine Hoggan, artist, for her delightful drawings.

Dina Stramandinoli for her typing skills.

The knitters: Edna Lomas, Joan Eckersley, Ruth Rintoule, Ruth Tyrie.

Joan Jackson, master embroiderer.

John Cummins of Queanbeyan Books for his constant search for lace knitting patterns.

Effie Nicholas, and DMC Needlecraft Pty Ltd, for their continued interest in our work and for supplying the DMC yarns used in producing the articles for the book.

My appreciation to the following for their assistance: Roslyn Panetta, Anne Savage, Michael Roath, Maurine Rogers, Patsy Ranger, Carol Davey, Patricia Wain, Patricia Walsh, Amelia Favretto, April Hersey, Pauline Kirk, Keith Hewitt, Alice Cottee, Vilma Tagliapietra, Alexis McLachlan, Margaret Hutchings, Sue Swart and Hilary Donelly.

Technical note

All the photographs in this book were taken using:

Kodak Ektachrome E100VS, Professional, 35mm daylight slide film

Zeiss Ikon/Voigtländer ICAREX 35S camera with Carl Zeiss ULTRON 50mm, f1.8 lens (bought in 1970)

First published in Australia in 2001 by Kangaroo Press
an imprint of Simon & Schuster (Australia) Pty Limited
20 Barcoo Street, East Roseville NSW 2069

A Viacom Company
Sydney New York London Toronto Tokyo Singapore

© Furze Hewitt 2001

National Library of Australia
Cataloguing-in-Publication data

Hewitt, Furze.

Aromatic gifts in classic knitted cotton

   Bibliography.
   Includes index.
   ISBN 0 7318 0896 7

   1. Gifts. 2. Potpourris (scented floral mixtures).
   3. Knitting – Patterns. I. Title

745.5

Cover design: Anna Soo Design
Illustrator: Josephine Hoggan
Photographer: Robert Roach

Set in Bembo 10.5/14
Printed in China by Everbest Printing Co

10 9 8 7 6 5 4 3 2 1

Contents

Introduction

If you enjoy knitting lace you can now discover the delight in creating aromatic gifts in the delicate beauty of white cotton knitting.

The patterns for the gifts, all from old publications, have been worked by knitters anxious to preserve them for future generations. Most are reproduced exactly as the originals (although translated into modern knitting terminology), while other designs have been adapted to suit the needs of a sachet. The knitters' work is acknowledged throughout the book in the captions.

Edna Lomas of Hamilton in Victoria excels in lace knitting. Edna designed the impressive Radiating Circles on page 37. Ruth Rintoule of Lalor in Victoria was the designer and knitter of the Ring Cushion with the intricate wide edging shown on page 40. Joan Eckersley of Soldiers Point in New South Wales created the exquisite Crazy Patchwork Pillow on page 39 with its knitted lace embellishments. Ruth Tyrie of Canberra knitted the practical Leaves and Squares cushion sachet on page 59.

Joan Jackson of Queanbeyan in New South Wales has displayed her gift as an embroiderer on many of the sachets. Whitby and Obsidian, shown on page 18, are both fine examples of what can be achieved in a combination of knitted lace and exquisite needlework.

Josephine Hoggan of Canberra supplied the delicate drawings scattered throughout the pages.

Robert Roach of Canberra once again displays his exceptional skill as a photographer, enhancing the knitted pieces, and allowing the intricacies of the patterns to be clearly seen.

The gifts cover a wide selection from a simple lavender sack to the beautiful Basket cushion.

The half dolls featured are from the 1930–40 period. Half dolls were originally designed to grace the tops of tea cosies, crumb whisks and so on. Those illustrated are now enjoying a new lease of life as useful and decorative lavender sachets. The dolls can also serve as pincushions and hat-pin holders. Half dolls can still be found, but if your search for originals is unsuccessful reproductions are available. See Suppliers, page 94.

All the patterns are suitable for knitters of moderate skill and require little sewing or assembly, and each could be used in many ways – don't limit your use of the patterns by merely following the ways in which I have used them.

Happy knitting!

Furze Hewitt

Abbreviations and Terms

Abbreviations are used in knitting instructions to save space, and to make the pattern easier to follow. It is important to read, and understand, the abbreviations before beginning to knit a pattern.

In this book most of the patterns use standard British abbreviations.

Some Helpful Abbreviations

k	knit
p	purl
st	stitch
sts	stitches
b	back
f	front
sl	slip
wyib	with yarn in back
wyif	with yarn in front
tog	together
*m1	make one stitch by winding yarn round needle
turn	work is turned before end of row
dpn	double pointed needle
motif	design unit
st st	stocking stitch—knit right side, purl wrong side
garter st	knit all rows
mb	make bobble
beg	beginning
psso	pass slipped stitch over
p2sso	pass 2 slipped stitches over
p-wise	purlwise
k-wise	knitwise
tbl	through back of loop
ybk	yarn back
yfwd	yarn forward
yon	yarn over needle
yrn	yarn around needle
R.H.	right hand
L.H.	left hand
tw st	twist stitch
inc	increase
dc	double crochet
ch	chain

* In old knitting publications the increase in laceknitting was referred to in several different ways ie. o – over. m1 – make one, and cast up.

In ordinary knitting the made stitches consist of the following:

y fwd	between two knit stitches.
yon	between a purl and knit action.
yrn	between two purl actions

In this book the above actions are referred to as m1– make one, as they were commonly written in old lace patterns.

COMPARATIVE TERMS

British	American
cast off	bind off
tension	gauge
alternate rows	every other row
miss	skip
work straight	work even
stocking stitch	stockinette stitch
shape cap	shape top

KNITTING NEEDLE SIZES

Metric	British	American
2 mm	14	00
2.25	13	0
2.75	12	1
3	11	2
3.25	10	3
3.75	9	4
4	8	5
4.5	7	6
5	6	7
5.5	5	8
6	4	9
6.5	3	10
7	2	10½
7.5	1	11
8	0	12
9	00	13
10	000	15

Techniques

Casting on

1 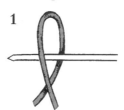 2 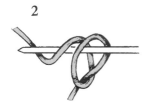 3 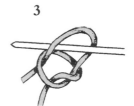 4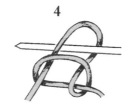

Thumb method

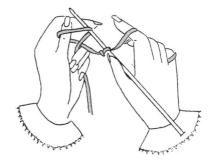 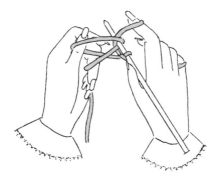 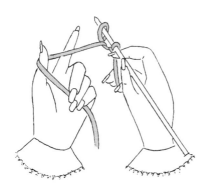

How to knit

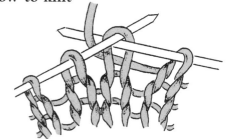

How to purl

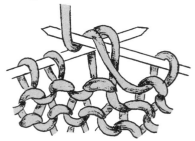

INVISIBLE CAST ON METHOD

1. Using contrasting thread, cast on the number of stitches required, work two rows in stocking stitch
2. With main thread, continue work until length required.
3. When work is completed, remove contrasting thread. Either graft or sew together open stitches from both ends of work.

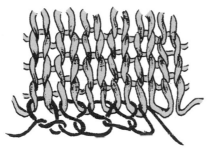

Invisible casting-on

INCREASING IN LACE KNITTING

There are three methods of increasing the number of stitches on a row, or in a round. One way is to knit twice into a stitch (Fig. 1). This increase can be worked k-wise or p-wise. Read your pattern carefully and work as directed.

A second method is to pick up a loop between two sts, and knit into that loop (Fig. 2). This prevents a hole in the knitting.

The third method, make one (or m1), produces the holes in lace knitting. The way it is worked depends on whether the extra stitch is to be made between two knit stitches, a knit and a purl, or two purl stitches. Between knit sts the yarn is brought forward, and over the needle as you knit the next stitch, thus forming a new stitch. Once again, read your pattern carefully.

Fig. 1

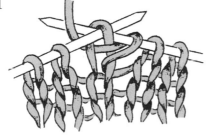

Fig. 2

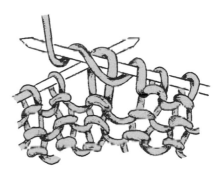

Fig. 3 (a) *Make one between two knit stitches.*

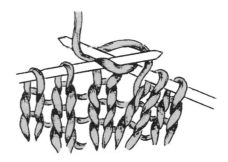

Fig. 3 (b) *Make one between two purl stitches.*

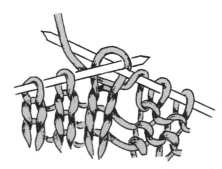

Fig. 3 (c) *Make one between a knit and a purl stitch.*

DECREASING IN LACE KNITTING

Again there are several methods. one method is to knit or purl two stitches together (Fig. 4 a and b). A second method is to pass the next but one stitch previously worked over the latter (Fig. 4 c and d).

Fig. 4

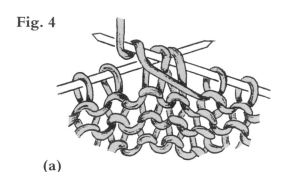

(a)

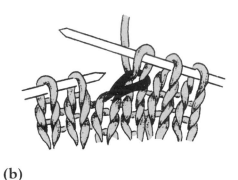

(b)

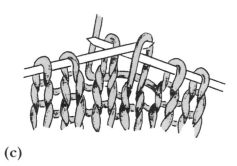

(c)

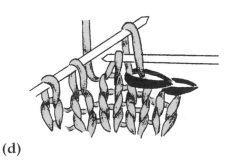

(d)

KNITTED PICOT CAST OFF

Knit 1st st. *sl 1 st from R.H. needle on to L.H. needle. Insert needle into this st cast on 2 sts, then cast off 5 sts. Repeat from * until all sts have been cast off.

KNITTING OFF YOUR STITCHES IF YOU CAN'T CROCHET

K1, *k2 tog, m1, k2 tog, turn. P1, *(k1, pl) twice, k1 * in next st.

P1, sl 1 purlwise, turn. Cast off 7 sts (1 st left on R.H. needle) *.

Repeat from *—* to last 5 sts. K3 tog, m1, k2 tog, turn, p1 (k1, p1) twice, k1, in next st, pl, sl 1 purlwise, turn. Cast off remaining sts.

For a larger loop on your edging, make 9 sts instead of 5 sts described above.

GRAFTING

A simplified method from Barbara Hosking

Place two needles, each with an equal number of sts, wrong sides together.

Thread bodkin with matching yarn. Insert bodkin k-wise into first st on front needle, slip off. Insert bodkin into second st p-wise, leave on needle. Insert bodkin through first st on back needle p-wise, slip off. Thread through second st k-wise, leave on needle. Repeat thus until grafting is completed.

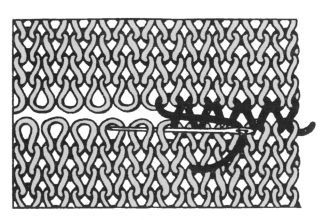

Grafting

TENSION

Experienced knitters know if their tension varies from the average. Early knitting instructions rarely have given tensions. The chart below is a basic guide to assist knitters of average tension.

Basic tension table gives average tension in st st over 25 mm (1")

Needle size	2-ply	3-ply	4-ply
12	9 sts	8½ sts	8 sts
11	8½ sts	8 sts	7½ sts
10	8 sts	7½ sts	7 sts
9	7½ sts	7 sts	6½ sts
8	7 sts	6½ sts	6 sts
7	6½ sts	6 sts	5½ sts

Lace knitters rely on their choice of yarn and needles and on the weight of the article being knitted, and adjust their knitting materials accordingly.

Suggested needles and cotton

Tray cloths, table cloths, small items of napery: Needles 2 mm (14), cotton 20

Lingerie: Needles 1.75 mm (15), cottons 30-40

Infants' wear, lawn, linen, Liberty cottons: Needles 1.25 mm (18), cottons 80-100

Handkerchiefs, fine voiles and baptistes: Needles 1.00 mm (20), cottons 80-100

Potpourri and lavender

LAVENDER

Pick the lavender heads before they come into full bloom, early in the day before the sun has drawn the aroma from the flowers. Spread the flower heads in a cool airy place to dry. When dry, rub the tiny flowers from the stalks. Retain the stalks to make aromatic faggots for the fire, or as an addition for pets' pillows. I grow several varieties of lavender in my garden, including *Lavandula vera*, *L. spica* and *L. officinalis* 'Alba'; all are suitable for drying. Colin Bates (see Suppliers, page 78) markets a variety of English lavender with a high oil content which makes it ideal for drying and potpourri. It has been named *L.* 'Margret Rocky Hall'.

Knitted lace is ideal for lavender sacks and sachets, as the open texture of the lace allows the aroma to freely escape.

BASIC POTPOURRI MIXTURE

For a change from lavender, complete your sachets with a potpourri of flowers from your garden. Rose petals, a little lavender, heliotrope, jasmine, honeysuckle, freesias, scented geranium leaves, lemon verbena (*Aloysia triphylla*), melissa, lime or orange blossoms, rosemary, mint – any or all of these make attractive potpourri. Collect the flowers and leaves on a dry day. Spread them over a gauze or wire frame and leave in a dry, well ventilated place to dry until crisp to the touch, stirring the material occasionally.

You will need to add a fixative to the dried material. To approximately ten handfuls of dried flowers and leaves I add a half cup of powdered or granulated orris root and a half cup of sea salt. Mix well, add just a few drops of lavender or rose oil (not enough to risk oil marks on the sachet fabric), and place in a paper bag or ceramic crock to ripen for about ten days. Plastic containers are unsuitable as they do not 'breathe' and tend to cause a moisture build-up, which can lead to mould developing in the potpourri.

The addition of a little cinnamon bark, a few cloves or a bay leaf gives the potpourri a warm, spicy aroma.

Leave out any large flowers and leaves when you are filling smaller inserts, especially for a sachet which is to go under a pillow.

Sachets and sachet inserts

To avoid repeating instructions *ad nauseum* with each pattern, here are instructions for a basic cushion-type sachet, which can be adapted to suit square, rectangular and round sachets with fabric faces, and a knitted base with fabric insert to suit the half dolls which feature throughout the book. A flat insert is preferable for square and oblong sachets.

Knitted lace, no matter how fine, is unsuitable by itself to contain fine, prickly, dried lavender flowers, or even a floral potpourri with its larger pieces, thus for each knitted sachet you will need to make a sachet insert to contain the aromatic material. This can be a simple drawstring bag made of fine net, muslin or organza which can be easily refilled when the aroma fades.

Note that the measurements given in this book are approximate only. The size of any sachet will vary according to your choice of yarn and needles, and the tension of the individual knitter. The amount of filling also affects the size. Avoid over-filling as it distorts the shape. Sleep pillows in particular should be only loosely filled so that they sit unobtrusively beneath the pillow to provide comfort and relaxation and allow the aroma to escape.

FABRIC-FACED SACHET

Cut a piece of fabric twice as long as the embroidered front of the cushion sachet, plus seam allowances, plus seam allowances for top and bottom of strip. Hem the two short ends.

Overlap these ends behind the sachet front until you have a square.

With right sides facing, stitch the embroidered front and the back together, then carefully turn right side out. Press lightly, avoiding the embroidery. Place the potpourri or lavender insert in sachet through lapped opening.

This method of closure enables the aromatic insert to be removed easily for replenishing. Circular and rectangular sachets can also made following this basic method.

KNITTED BASE FOR HALF DOLL

Materials
DMC Hermina cotton

Pair needles 2 mm (14)

Fine net

Lavender or potpourri

Fibre filling

Cast on 40 sts.

Row 1: Knit to last st. Turn.

Row 2: Sl 1, knit to last st. Turn.

Rows 3 and 4: Knit to last 2 sts. Turn.

Rows 5 and 6: Knit to last 3 sts. Turn.

Continue working this way until 10 sts remain at both ends of row. Knit to end of row.

Repeat until 8 sections are completed.

Cast off.

Fill the base lightly with soft fibre filling. Insert net sachet filled with lavender or potpourri. Close the seam as neatly as possible. Run a thread around top of cylindrical base. Insert half doll into hole at top. Stitch firmly through holes in the base of the doll, using a strong thread and making sure the doll is securely attached to the base. You can vary the base by the addition of discs of white card 8 cm (3 inches) in diameter. The discs can be placed at the bottom of the sphere before filling, making a firm and stable base for your half doll. The doll and base are now ready to be enhanced with knitted lace.

The size of the base can be adjusted by the use of different yarns and needles. I generally make the base in white, but coloured yarn can create an interesting effect.

CIRCULAR UNDERSKIRT FOR HALF DOLL

Cut a circle of fine white fabric approximately 50 cm (20 inches) in diameter (or other size required). Hand or machine stitch 2 rows of gathering stitches around circle. Gently draw up the circle. Before tying around doll's waist, insert fibre fill and a generous sachet of lavender or potpourri. Insert the half doll, tighten the gathering threads, and fix the underskirt to the doll by stitching through the holes in the doll with a strong thread.

For a bouffant skirt, as worn by Cressida, Perdita and Winsome (page 60), add a net overskirt to lift the knitted lace. The overskirt is simply a generous strip of net folded in half and gathered, drawn up and neatened at the waistline, and tied to secure in place. The knitted skirt is arranged over the top.

The Patterns

Amelia *(instructions on page 21)*

Three Lavender Sacks *(instructions on page 22)*

Delicate Lace Sachet *(instructions on page 24)*

Obsidian *(instructions on page 25)*   **Whitby** *(instructions on page 26)*

Flower Patch *(instructions on page 27)*

Crisp Honeycomb Sachet *(instructions on page 28)*

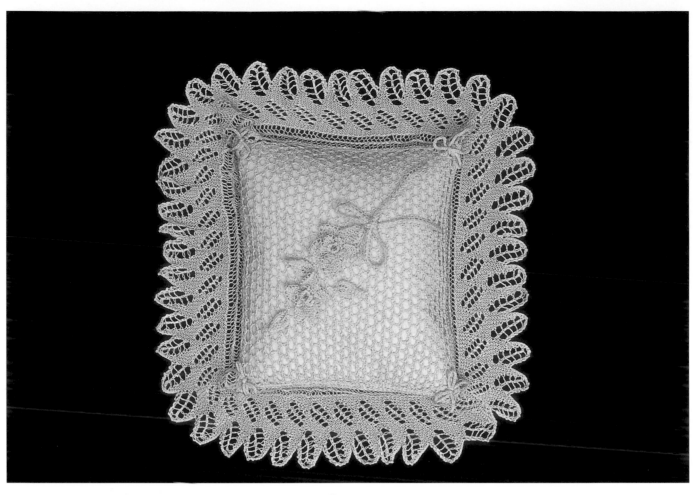

Patrician Lace Pillow *(instructions on page 29)*

Dandelion Clock Cushion *(instructions on page 31)*

Ellan Mesh Lace Cushion *(instructions on page 32)*

1

Amelia

A beautiful sleep sachet of Mountmellick work, designed and made by Joan Jackson, is edged with Dimity, a classic lace edging knitted by the author.

Materials

Piece of fine twill fabric of the size required

DMC Broder cotton in white and cream for a traditional look

1 × 20 g ball DMC 12 cotton

Pair needles 1.25 mm (18)

Lavender insert

Sewing needle and thread for attaching lace

Dimity edging

Cast on 9 sts.

Row 1: K3, k2 tog, m1, k2 tog, (m1, k1) twice.

Row 2 and alternate Rows: Knit.

Row 3: K2, (k2 tog, m1) twice, k3, m1, k1.

Row 5: K1, (k2 tog, m1) twice, k5, m1, k1.

Row 7: K3, (m1, k2 tog) twice, k1, k2 tog, m1, k2 tog.

Row 9: K4, m1, k2 tog, m1, k3 tog, m1, k2 tog.

Row 11: K5, m1, k3 tog, m1, k2 tog.

Row 12: Knit.

Repeat rows 1–12 until length desired.

Make a simple lined envelope sachet, closed size approximately 25 × 20 cm (10 × 8 inches). Joan embroidered the flap in a traditional Mountmellick design using white and cream DMC threads. Other types of embroidery such as candlewicking would give an interesting alternative.

Traditionally Mountmellick work was done on a twill-like jean fabric. The Amelia sachet is worked on an antique piece of this fabric. The classic edging is reminiscent of torchon lace, and the delicate sheen of the cotton thread enhances the work. Use embroidery books to help create your own designs (see Bibliography, page 94).

Press the sachet, avoiding the embroidery. Press the lace edging and attach to sachet with small stitches. Fill with lavender or a potpourri sleep mixture.

2

Three Lavender Sacks

(Pictured page 17.) Janina on the left is by Ruth Rintoule. Leaves, in the centre, is a distinctive design by Edna Lomas, and the Filet sack on the right is by the author. The mesh-like knitting is perfect for aromatic sacks. All three sacks reveal their grosgrain inner sacks in shades of lavender, and are tied with silk ribbons.

JANINA

Materials

1 × 10 g ball DMC 10 cotton

Pair needles 2.75 mm (12)

Cast on 72 sts. Knit 1 row.

Row 1: P2, *m1, p4 tog*. Repeat from * ending m1, p2.

Row 2: K2, *(k1, p1, k1) into m1 of previous row, k1. Repeat from * ending (k1, p1, k1) into m1 of previous row, k2.

Row 3: P2, *p4 tog, m1. Repeat from * ending p4 tog, p1.

Row 4: K2, *(k1, p1, k1) into m1 of previous row, k1. Repeat from * ending k2.

Repeat rows 1–4 until sack measures 14 mm (5½ inches), ending on row 4.

Knit 2 rows.

Cast off.

Stitch sides together leaving seam at back. Stitch across bottom of sack. Insert lavender. Tie with ribbons.

LEAVES

Materials

1 × 10 g ball DMC 10 cotton

Pair needles 2 mm (14)

Length of silk ribbon

Sewing needle and thread

Lavender

Cast on 31 sts. Knit one row.

Row 1: (Wrong side), k3, (p1, k5) to last 3 sts, k3.

Row 2: P3, (m1, k1, m1, p5) to last 3 sts, p3.

Row 3: K3, (p3, k5) to last 3 sts, k3.

Row 4: P3, (k1, m1, k1, m1, k1, p5) to last 3 sts, p3.

Row 5: K3, (p5, k5) to last 3 sts, k3.

Row 6: P3, (k2, m1, k1, m1, k2, p5) to last 3 sts, p3.

Row 7: K3, (p7, k5) to last 3 sts, k3.

Row 8: P3, (k7, p5) to last 3 sts, p3.

Row 9: As row 7.

Row 10: P3, (sl 1, k1, psso, k3, k2 tog, p5) to last 3 sts, p3.

Row 11: As row 5.

Row 12: P3, (sl 1, k1, psso, k1, k2 tog, p5) to last 3 sts, p3.

Row 13: As row 3.

Row 14: P3, (sl 1, k2 tog, psso, p5) to last 3 sts, p3.

Row 15: Knit.

Work 3 rows as follows:

Row 1: Knit.

Row 2: Purl.

Row 3: Knit.

Work pattern rows 1–15.

Work 3 rows as follows:

Row 1: Knit.

Row 2: Purl.

Row 3: (Right side facing), k1, k2 tog, k2, (k2 tog, k4) to last 2 sts, k2 tog (25 sts).

Continue as follows:

Row 1: K2, (p1, k4) to last 2 sts, k2.

Row 2: P2, (m1, k1, m1, p4) to last 2 sts, p2.

Row 3: K2, (p3, k4) to last 2 sts, k2.

Row 4: P2, (k1, m1, k1, m1, k1, p4) to last 2 sts, p2.

Row 5: K2, (p5, k4) to last 2 sts, k2.

Row 6: P2 tog, (k2, m1, k1, m1, k2, p1, p2 tog, p1) to last 7 sts, k2, m1, k1, k1, m1, k2, p2 tog.

Row 7: K1, (p7, k3) to last st, k1.

Row 8: P1, (k7, p2 tog, p1) to last 8 sts, k7, p1.

Row 9: K1, (p7, k2) to last st, k1.

Row 10: P1, (sl 1, k1, psso, k3, k2 tog, p2 tog) to last st, p1.

Row 11: K1, (p5, k1) to end of row.

Row 12: P1, (sl 1, k1, psso, k1, k2 tog, p1) to end of row.

Row 13: K1, (p3, k1) to end of row.

Row 14: P1, (sl 1, k2 tog, psso, p1) to end of row.

Row 15: Knit.

Repeat rows 1–15. Purl one row. Cast off.

Join the sides and bottom of the sack. Make insert in contrasting colour. Tie matching silk ribbon around neck of sack.

FILET SACK

Materials

1 × 10 g ball DMC 10 cotton

Pair needles 2 mm (14)

Length of silk ribbon

Fabric in contrasting colour for inner sack

Lavender

Cast on 39 sts (or multiples of 3 in width required).

Row 1: (Right side of work), k2, (sl 2, pass first slipped st over 2nd st and off needle. Sl 1, pass 2nd slipped st over 3rd st and off needle. Slip the 3rd slipped stitch st back onto L.H. needle, m2. Knit the 3rd slipped st in usual fashion). Repeat to last st, k1 (39 sts).

Row 2: K3, (p1, k2) to end of row.

Repeat rows 1–2 until sack measures 14 cm (5½ inches).

Make another side in the same fashion.

To make up

Carefully stitch the bottom and sides together. Insert fabric sachet containing lavender. Tie a double ribbon around the neck of the sack.

3

Delicate Lace Sachet

A lavender sachet made from a hemstitched linen handkerchief, and edged with fine lace. Beautifully knitted by Joan Eckersley.

Materials

Fine linen handkerchief

1 × 20 g ball DMC 80 cotton

Pair needles 1.25 mm (18)

Embroidery thread

Narrow silk ribbon

Fine muslin for lavender and wadding insert

Sewing needle and thread

Cast on 19 sts. Knit one row.

Row 1: K2, (m1, k2 tog) twice, k6, k2 tog, m1, k3, m1, k2.

Row 2: K2, m1, k5, m1, k2 tog, k6, (m1, k2 tog) twice, k1.

Row 3: K2, (m1, k2 tog) twice, k4, k2 tog, m1, k1, k2 tog, m1, k1, m1, k2 tog, k1, m1, k2.

Row 4: K2, m1, k1, k2 tog, m1, k3, m1, k2 tog, k1, m1, k2 tog, k4, (m1, k2 tog) twice, k1.

Row 5: K2, (m1, k2 tog) twice, k2, k2 tog, m1, k1, k2 tog, m1, k5, m1, k2 tog, k1, m1, k2.

Row 6: K2, m1, k1, k2 tog, m1, k3, m1, k2 tog, k2, m1, k2 tog, k1, m1, k2 tog, k2, (m1, k2 tog) twice, k1.

Row 7: K2, (m1, k2 tog) twice, k3, m1, k2 tog, k1, m1, k2 tog, k3, k2 tog, (m1, k1, k2 tog) twice.

Row 8: Cast off 1st. (K1, m1, k2 tog) twice, (k1, k2 tog, m1) twice, k5, (m1, k2 tog) twice, k1.

Row 9: K2, (m1, k2 tog) twice, k5, m1, k2 tog, k1, m1, sl 1, k2 tog, psso, m1, (k1, k2 tog) twice.

Row 10: K2, m1, k2 tog, k3, k2 tog, m1, k7, (m1, k2 tog) twice, k1.

Row 11: K2, (m1, k2 tog) twice, k7, m1, k2 tog, k1, k2 tog, m1, k3.

Row 12: Cast off 2 sts. K1, m1, k3 tog, m1, k9, (m1, k2 tog) twice, k1.

Repeat rows 1–12 until length desired.

Cast off.

Press lightly.

Fold handkerchief thus:
Embroider a rose or two for the ends of opening. Attach lace along opening, as indicated on the diagram.

Make a fine muslin insert to fit, line with a piece of sheet wadding, and insert a flat lavender sachet. Trim with bows and extra flowers if desired.

4

Obsidian

A Victorian style sachet, its richly coloured embroidery enhanced by the black background and the knitted lace. Embroidery by Joan Jackson, lace by the author.

Materials

• OBSIDIAN LACE
2 × 5 g balls DMC Special Dentelle 80 cotton, noir
Pair needles 1.25 mm (18)
Fine sewing thread and needle for attaching lace to sachet
Black fabric for basic circular sachet (see page 13)
Embroidery in DMC threads 115, 434, 335, 340, 725, 742, 776, 826, 827, 971, 3746, 3363
Metallic gold thread

• LACE BRAID
1 × 20 g ball DMC Cordonnet Special 10 cotton
Pair needles 1.75 mm (15)

Lace edging

Cast on 20 sts.
Row 1: Sl 1, k3, (m1, k2 tog) 7 times, m1, k2.
Row 2: Knit.
Row 3: Sl 1, k14, (m1, k2 tog) twice, m1, k2.

Row 4: K7, p2. Turn.
Row 5: K3, (m1, k2 tog) twice, m1, k2.
Row 6: K7, p12. Turn.
Row 7: Knit.
Row 8: Cast off 3 sts. Knit to end of row.

Repeat rows 1–8 until length desired to edge sachet, allowing extra fullness at corners if trimming a square or rectangular shape.

Cast off.

Lace braid

A one-row pattern.
Cast on 3 sts.
M1, k2 tog, k1.
Repeat this row until length desired.
Cast off.

To make up

Press the lace, attach to the sachet with tiny stiches. Stitch lace braid around the embroidered centre for a neat finish.

Trim with ribbons as required.

5

Whitby

Another beautiful example of exquisite embroidery by Joan Jackson. Lace and braid by the author.

Materials

• WHITBY LACE
2 × 5 g balls DMC Special Dentelle 80 cotton, noir
Pair needles 1.25 mm (18)
Fine sewing thread and needle for attaching lace to sachet
Black linen for basic circular sachet (see page 13)
Embroidery in DMC threads in colours as follows:
2-ply Medici Wool 94, 8720
No.8 Pearl 90
Rayon 307, 349
DMC stranded cottons 102, 104, 106, 108, 115, 91, 300, 501, 523, 972, 973, 986

• LACE BRAID
1 × 20 g ball DMC Cordonnet Special 10 cotton
Pair needles 1.75 mm (15)

Lace edging

Cast on 26 sts.
Row 1: K15, (k2 tog, m1) twice, k3, m2, k2 tog, m2, k2.
Row 2: K3, (p1, k2) twice, p15. Turn.
Row 3: K9, (k2 tog, m1) twice, k11.

Row 4: K2, m2, k2 tog, k1, k2 tog, m2, k2 tog, k1, p14, k5.
Row 5: K13, (k2 tog, m1) twice, k5, p1, k4, p1, k2.
Row 6: K12, p13. Turn.
Row 7: P10, (m1, k2 tog) twice, k2, k2 tog, m2, sl 1, k2 tog, psso, m2, (k2 tog) twice.
Row 8: K3, p1, k2, p1, k3, p4, k15.
Row 9: K5, p11, (m1, k2 tog) twice, k9.
Row 10: Cast off 3 sts. K5, p4, k11. Turn.
Row 11: P12, (m1, k2 tog) twice, k5.
Row 12: K5, p4, k17.
Repeat rows 1–12 until length desired.

Lace braid

A one-row pattern.
Cast on 3 sts.
M1, k2 tog, k1.
Repeat this row until length desired.
Cast off.

To make up

Press lace lightly, avoiding the fluted section. Attach to sachet with tiny stitches. Add lace braid around embroidered centre. Trim with ribbon if desired.

6

Flower Patch

An embroidered boudoir cushion in cream silk dupion. Designed and made by Joan Jackson. The lace was knitted by the author to frame the embroidery.

Materials

1 × 20 g ball DMC 10 cotton, ecru

Pair needles 2 mm (14)

Sewing needle and ecru cotton

Lace measures 2.5 cm (1inch)

Cast on 7 sts.

Row 1: Knit.

Row 2: Purl.

Row 3: Sl 1 purlwise, k2, m1 k2 tog, m2, k2 tog.

Row 4: M1, k2, p1, k2, m1, k2 tog, k1.

Row 5: Sl 1 purlwise, k2, m1, k2 tog, k4.

Row 6: K6, m1, k2 tog, k1.

Row 7: Sl 1 purlwise, k2, m1, k2 tog, (m2, k2 tog) twice.

Row 8: (K2, p1) twice, k2, m1, k2 tog, k1.

Row 9: Sl 1 purlwise, k2, m1, k2 tog, k6.

Row 10: K8, m1, k2 tog, k1.

Row 11: Sl 1 purlwise, k2, m1, k2 tog, (m2, k2 tog) 3 times.

Row 12: (K2, p1) 3 times, k2, m1, k2 tog, k1.

Row 13: Sl 1 purlwise, k2, m1, k2 tog, k9.

Row 14: Cast off 7 sts. K3, m1, k2 tog, k1.

Repeat rows 3–14 until length desired. Cast off.

Lightly press lace. Attach to cushion to frame the embroidery.

7

Crisp Honeycomb Sachet

An interesting sachet designed and knitted by the author with a beautifully embroidered knob by Joan Jackson. This sachet would make an attractive hat-pin holder or pincushion. Glass holder by Peter Crisp (see Suppliers, page 94).

Materials

Lavender base (see page 13)

Honeycomb overskirt (knitted in 2 pieces)

Embroidered knob

Green ribbon

Lavender

Fibre filling

2 × 8 cm (3 inch) discs of white cardboard

Sewing needle and cotton

Honeycomb overskirt

(make 2)

Cast on 42 sts.

Row 1: K1, (m1, p4 tog) to last st, k1.

Row 2: K1, [k1, (k1, p1, k1) in m1 of previous row] to last st, k1.

Row 3: Knit.

Repeat rows 1–3 ten times or until length desired.

Cast off.

Sew the side seams carefully. Thread white cotton through top of sachet. Draw up to fit top. Make a decorative knob, outline in ribbon leaves. Lightly tack ribbon into place so that the honeycomb top can be removed for laundering.

To assemble the base

Insert one of the cardboard discs in the bottom of base (to hold bottom firm). Fill with fibre filling and lavender insert. Stitch rear seam of base, inserting the cardboard disc at the top before closing the opening. With your hands, gently flatten at top and bottom of sachet. Add the honeycomb knitted cover.

8

Patrician Lace Pillow

A lace mesh aromatic pillow with wide lace edging and knitted trim. Designed and knitted by author. Courtesy Patricia Walsh.

Materials

• LACE MESH CENTRE

1 × 20 g DMC 20 cotton, ecru

Pair needles 1.75 mm (15)

Centre measurement: 20 cm × 24 cm (8 × 9½ inches)

• PILLOW EDGING

2 × 20 g DMC 20 cotton, ecru

Pair needles 1.75 mm (15)

Width of edging approximately 8 cm (3 inches)

• FLORAL SPRAY

1 × 20 g ball DMC 20 cotton, ecru

Small amount of DMC 100 cotton, ecru

2 pairs needles, 1 mm (20) and 2 mm (14)

Sewing thread in darker ecru for French knots

Length of lace chain for bow

Lace mesh centre

Cast on 60 sts.

Row 1: ★K4, m2. Repeat from ★ to last 4 sts, k4.

Row 2: K2, ★k2 tog, k1, p1 in next st, k2 tog. Repeat from ★. End k2 tog, k2.

Row 3: K2, m1, ★k4, m2. Repeat from ★ ending k4, m1, k2.

Row 4: K3, k2 tog, ★k2 tog, k1, p1 in next st, k2 tog. Repeat from ★ ending k2 tog, k3.

Repeat these 4 rows until length desired.

Cast off.

Lace edging

Cast on 24 sts.

Row 1: Sl 1, k2, m1, k2 tog, k1, m1, k2 tog, k2, (m1, k2 tog) twice, k5, (m2, k2 tog) twice, k1.

Row 2: K3, p1, k2, p1, k13, (m1, k2 tog, k1) twice.

Row 3: Sl 1, k2, m1, k2 tog, k1, m1, k2 tog, k3, (m1, k2 tog) twice, k6, (m2, k2 tog) twice, k1.

Row 4: K3, p1, k2, p1, k15, (m1, k2 tog, k1) twice.

Row 5: Sl 1, k2, m1, k2 tog, k1, m1, k2 tog, k4, (m1, k2 tog) twice, k7, (m2, k2 tog) twice, k1.

Row 6: K3, p1, k2, p1, k17, (m1, k2 tog, k1) twice.

Row 7: Sl 1, k2, m1, k2 tog, k1, m1, k2 tog, k5, (m1, k2 tog) twice, k8, (m2, k2 tog) twice, k1.

Row 8: K3, p1, k2, p1, k19, (m1, k2 tog, k1) twice.

Row 9: Sl 1, k2, m1, k2 tog, k1, m1, k2 tog, k6, (m1, k2 tog) twice, k9, (m2, k2 tog) twice, k1.

Row 10: K3, p1, k2, p1, k21, (m1, k2 tog, k1) twice.

Row 11: Sl 1, k2, m1, k2 tog, k1, m1, k2 tog, k26.

Row 12: Cast off 10 sts. K17, (m1, k2 tog, k1) twice.

Repeat rows 1–12 until length desired.

To make up, make basic cushion filled with fibre filling and lavender insert. Sew edging around mesh centre, allowing fullness at corners. Press slightly. Attach lace cover to basic aromatic cushion. Knit 4 lengths of fine cord. Tie into bows at each corner.

Floral spray

Make 2 flowers; each one is worked in 3 layers.

First layer

Cast on 2 sts.

Row 1: M1, knit to end.

Row 2: Sl 1, knit to end.

Repeat rows 1–2 until there are 9 sts on needle, ending with row 2.

Next Row: M1, k3 tog, knit to end.

Next Row: Sl 1, knit to end.

Repeat from row 1 until desired number of petals has been worked. Cast off.

Second layer

Work as first layer, increasing until petal has 7 sts, then

decreasing until 2 sts remain. Make the same number of petals as in first layer.

Cast off.

Third layer

Work as first and second layers until petal has 5 sts. Make 5 petals. Cast off.

To make up

Thread yarn through straight edge. Draw up to form circle. Stitch the 3 layers of petals together through the centre to form flower.

Centre of flower

Using DMC 100 cotton, ecru, and 1 mm (20) needles, work the centre thus:

Cast on 10 sts (make 2).

Row 1: K1, (m1, k1) to end of row.

Repeat row 1, twice.

Cast off.

Arrange to form a tiny rose-shaped centre. Stitch centre to the layered flower. Work French knots in a slightly darker shade in centre to complete.

Leaves

(make 3)

Cast on 3 sts.

Row 1: K1, (m1, k1) twice.

Row 2 and alternate Rows: Purl.

Row 3: K2, m1, k1, m1, k2.

Row 5: K3, m1, k1, m1, k3.

Row 7: K4, m1, k1, m1, k4.

Row 9: Knit.

Row 11: K4, sl 1, k2 tog, psso, k4.

Row 13: K3, sl 1, k2 tog, psso, k3.

Row 15: K2, sl 1, k2 tog, psso, k2.

Row 17: K1, sl 1, k2 tog, psso, k1.

Row 19: Sl 1, k2 tog, psso.

Cast off.

Lace chain bow

Cast on 2 sts.

Row 1: M1, p2 tog.

Repeat this row until length desired to tie into a generous bow.

Cast off.

Press carefully. Arrange the flowers, leaves and lace bow as illustrated or to suit your preference.

9

Dandelion Clock Cushion

The antique swirl medallion makes an attractive centre for this aromatic cushion. This effective swirl pattern, sometimes used with a connecting square, was popular in the nineteenth century. Cushion designed by author.

Materials

• CUSHION

1 m (40 inches) lavender linen

12 small guipure flowers

Sewing cotton to match fabric

Sewing needle

Cushion insert

Lavender

Cushion measures 31 cm (12 inches) square; the antique medallion is 18 cm (7 inches) in diameter

• THE SWIRL

1 × 20 g ball DMC 20 cotton

Set of four needles 2 mm (14)

Crochet hook 1.50 mm

Cast on 8 sts (3 on each of 2 needles, 2 on third needle).

Round 1: Knit.

Round 2: (M1, k1) 8 times.

Round 3: Knit.

Round 4: (M1, k1) 16 times.

Round 5: (K2, k2 tog) 8 times.

Round 6: (M1, k1, m1, k2 tog) 8 times.

Round 7: Knit (32 sts).

Round 8: [(M1, k1) twice, m1, k2 tog]. Repeat to end of round.

Round 9: (K4, k2 tog) 8 times.

Round 10: [(M1, k1) twice, m1, k1, k2 tog]. Repeat to end of round.

Round 11: (K5, k2 tog) 8 times.

Round 12: [(M1, k1) twice, m1, k2, k2 tog]. Repeat to end of round.

Round 13: (K6, k2 tog) 8 times.

Continue in this way, working one stitch more between the panels until the swirl is the size required.

Cast off with crochet hook (pick up 5 sts, sc, ch10) to end. Fasten off.

Press the work. Lightly spray with starch, press again under a cloth. Pin out to form circle and allow to dry.

Make up basic cushion. Sew knitted swirl into centre. Add three small flowers in each corner if desired. Add lavender insert and cushion filling.

10

Ellan Mesh Lace Cushion

An aromatic cushion in a delightful mesh design with an edging from a 1912 pattern. The cushion was designed and knitted by the author. Courtesy Anne Savage.

Materials

1 × 50 g ball DMC 10 cotton, ecru

Pair needles 2 mm (14)

4 buttons

4 tassels

Basic cushion 18 cm (7 inches) square with fibre filling and lavender insert

Sewing needle and ecru thread

Finished cushion is approximately 30 cm (12 inches) square

Centre mesh

Cast on 48 sts.

Row 1: Wrong side, (k2 tog, m2, k2 tog) to end of row.

Row 2: Knit, (working k1, p1, in each m2 of previous row).

Row 3: K2, (k2 tog, m2, k2 tog) to last 2 sts, k2.

Row 4: Knit, (working k1, p1, in each m2 of previous row).

Repeat rows 1–4 until length desired.

Edging

Cast on 14 sts.

Row 1: Sl 1, k2, m1, p2 tog, k2, m2, (k2 tog) twice, m2, k3.

Row 2: Cast on 2 sts. Cast off 1 st. K4, p1, k3, p1, k2, m1, p2 tog, k3.

Row 3: Sl 1, k2, m1, p2 tog, k1, (k2 tog) twice, m2, (k2 tog) twice, m2, k3.

Row 4: Cast on 2 sts. Cast off 1 st. K4, p1, k3, p1, k3, m1, p2 tog, k3.

Row 5: Sl 1, k2, m1, p2 tog, k2, m2, (k2 tog) twice, m2, (k2 tog) twice, m2, k3.

Row 6: Cast on 2 sts. Cast off 1 st. K4, (p1, k3) twice, p1, k2, m1, p2 tog, k3.

Row 7: Sl 1, k2, m1, p2 tog, k1, (k2 tog) twice, m2, (k2 tog) twice, m2, (k2 tog) twice, m2, k3.

Row 8: Cast on 2 sts. Cast off 1 st. K4, (p1, k3) 3 times, m1, p2 tog, k3.

Row 9: Sl 1, k2, m1, p2 tog, k2, [(m2, (k2 tog) twice)] 3 times, m2, k3.

Row 10: Cast on 1 st. Cast off 1 st. (K3, p1) 4 times, k2, m1, p2 tog, k3.

Row 11: Sl 1, k2, m1, p2 tog, k1, (k2 tog) twice, [(m2, (k2 tog) twice)] 3 times, k2 tog.

Row 12: Cast on 1 st. Cast off 1 st. (K3, p1) 3 times, k3, m1, p2 tog, k3.

Row 13: Sl 1, k2, m1, p2 tog, k2, [(m2, (k2 tog) twice)] 3 times, k2 tog.

Row 14: Cast on 1 st. Cast off 1 st. (K3, p1) 3 times, k2, m1, p2 tog, k3.

Row 15: Sl 1, k2, m1, p2 tog, k1, (k2 tog) twice, m2, (k2 tog) twice, m2, (k2 tog) 3 times.

Row 16: Cast on 1 st. Cast off 1 st. (K3, p1) twice, k3, m1, p2 tog, k3.

Row 17: Sl 1, k2, m1, p2 tog, k2, m2, (k2 tog) twice, m2, (k2 tog) 3 times.

Row 18: Cast on 1 st. Cast off 1 st. (K3, p1) twice, k2, m1, p2 tog, k3.

Row 19: Sl 1, k2, m1, p2 tog, k1, (k2 tog) twice, m2, (k2 tog) 3 times.

Row 20: Cast on 2 sts. Cast off 1 st. K4, p1, k3, m1, p2 tog, k3.

Repeat rows 1–20 until length desired, casting off on row 18.

To make up

Sew edging around mesh centre, easing gently around the corners. Sew a button on each corner of the basic cushion. Place the knitted cover over the basic cushion, bringing the buttons through at each corner. Hang a tassel on each button. The cover is easily removed for laundering.

11

Radiating Circles

A decorative pattern which can be used to create various items such as the bowl, vase, sachets and plate illustrated here. Edna Lomas knitted these charming pieces.

Materials

1 × 20 g ball DMC 20 cotton

Set of 5 double-pointed needles 2 mm (14)

Stiffening for circles (see end of pattern for method)

Cast on 8 sts (2 sts on each of 4 needles). Work with 5th needle.

Round 1: Knit.

Round 2: (M1, k into f & b of next st) to end of round (24 sts).

Round 3: (k & p into made st, k2) to end of round.

Round 4: Sl 1st st from L.H. needle onto R.H. needle at the start of each needle in the round. (M1, sl 1, k1, psso, k2 tog) to end of round. Repeat rounds 3 and 4 twice.

Round 9: (K1, p1, k1, p1 into made st, k2) to end of round.

Rounds 10–12: Knit.

Round 13: (M1, k2) to end of round.

Round 14: As round 3.

Round 15: As round 4.

Repeat rounds 14 and 15 eight times.

Round 32: (K1, p1, k1 into made st, k2) to end of round.

Round 33–35: Knit.

Round 36: (M1, k2) to end of round.

Change to circular needle if preferred.

Round 37: As round 3.

Round 38: Sl 1st st from L.H. needle onto R.H. needle at beginning of round, (m1, sl 1, k1, psso, k2 tog) to end of round.

Repeat rounds 37 and 38 thirteen times.

Round 65: (K1, p1, k1, p1, k1 into made st, p2 tog) to end of round.

Round 66: Purl.

Cast off in crochet as follows:

Insert hook into 1st st on L.H. needle and draw up a loop, sl st off L.H. needle, (1ch 1dc into next st on L.H. needle). Repeat, ending with 1ch then 1 sl st into 1st st.

Fasten off.

Use knitted cast-off if you prefer (see page 10).

Lightly press the work.

To stiffen a piece follow the mixing directions on a powdered starch packet. Place the wet piece over the desired shape, and allow to dry. (For average stiffness allow 1 heaped tablespoon of powdered starch to 600 ml of cold water.)

12

Five Round Sachets

(Pictured page 37.) Clockwise from bottom left these Round sachets are named Star, Cyclamen, Leaf, Diamond and Victoria. Star is a ten-pointed star sachet, 18 cm (7 inches) in diameter, designed and knitted by Edna Lomas. Cyclamen is a dainty sachet 18 cm (7 inches) in diameter made by Edna Lomas, finished with tiny beads and an antique embroidered button in the centre. Leaf is a delicate sleep sachet by Edna Lomas, its 15 cm (6 inch) size ideal to tuck under the pillow. Diamond, adapted and knitted by Ruth Rintoule from an 1897 pattern, is 18 cm (7 inches) in diameter. Victoria, a small sachet approximately 13 cm (5 inches) in diameter, decorated with a knitted cord bow, was knitted by Edna Lomas from a Victorian motif pattern.

STAR

Materials

1 × 50 g ball DMC 20 cotton

Set of 4 double-pointed needles 2 mm (14)

Crochet hook 1.50 mm

Sewing needle and thread

Basic 18 cm (7 inch) lavender cushion

Finely knitted cord bow for centre

Cast on 10 sts (3 sts on each of 2 needles, 4 sts on 3rd needle). Work with 4th needle.

Round 1: Knit.

Round 2: (M1, k1) to end of round.

Round 3 and alternate Rounds: Knit.

Round 4: (M1, k2) to end of round.

Round 6: (M1, k3) to end of round.

Round 8: (M1, k4) to end of round.

Round 10: (M1, k5) to end of round.

Round 12: (M1, k6) to end of round.

Round 14: (M1, k7) to end of round.

Round 16: (M1, k8) to end of round.

Round 18: (M1, k1, m1, sl 1, k1, psso, k6) to end of round (100 sts).

Round 20: (M1, k3, m1, sl 1, k1, psso, k5) to end of round.

Round 22: (M1, k5, m1, sl 1, k1, psso, k4) to end of round.

Round 24: (M1, k7, m1, sl 1, k1, psso, k3) to end of round.

Round 26: (M1, k1, m1, sl 1, k1, psso, k3, k2 tog, m1, k1, m1, sl 1, k1, psso, k2,) to end of round.

Round 28: (M1, k3, m1, sl 1, k1, psso, k1, k2 tog, m1, k3, m1, sl 1, k1, psso, k1) to end of round.

Round 30: (M1, k5, m1, sl 1, k2 tog, psso, m1, k5, m1, sl 1, k1, psso) to end of round.

Round 32: (M1, k3, k2 tog, k2, m1, k1, m1, k2, k2 tog, k3, m1, k1) to end of round.

Cast off loosely, press the work.

With crochet hook make 1sc in next st, (cl 5, 1sc in 5th cl from hook, miss 3, 1sc in next st). Repeat around edge. Join crochet. Fasten off or cast off knitwise (see page 10).

CYCLAMEN

Materials

1 × 50 g ball DMC 20 cotton

Set of 4 double-pointed needles 2 mm (14)

Needle and thread for sewing sachet

Button for centre if desired

Sachet measures 18 cm (7 inches)

Cast on 6 sts (2 sts on each of 3 needles). Work with 4th needle.

Round 1: Knit.

Round 2: (M1, k1 tbl) to end of round (12 sts).

Round 3 and alternate Rounds: Knit.

Round 4: (M1, k1, m1, k1 tbl) to end of round (24 sts).

Round 6: (M1, k3, m1, k1 tbl) to end of round (36 sts).

Round 8: (M1, k2 tog, m1, k1, m1, sl 1, k1, psso, m1, k1 tbl) to end of round (48 sts).

Round 10: (K2 tog, m1, k3, m1, sl 1, k1, psso, k1 tbl) to end of round.

NB Before commencing round 12, knit 1st st from 1st needle onto 3rd needle and similarly sl 1st st of 2nd and 3rd needles onto ends of previous needles (this action, knit one right, will be referred to as kir).

Round 12: (M1, k2 tog, m1, k1 tbl, m1, sl 1, k1, psso, m1, sl 1, k2 tog, psso) to end of round.

Round 14: (M1, k2, m1, sl 1, k2 tog, psso, m1, k2, m1, k1 tbl) to end of round (60 sts).

Round 16: (M1, k3, m1, sl 1, k2 tog, psso, m1, k3, m1, k1 tbl) to end of round (72 sts).

Round 18: (M1, k4, m1, sl 1, k2 tog, psso, m1, k4, m1, k1 tbl) to end of round (84 sts).

Round 20: (M1, k5, m1, sl 1, k2 tog, psso, m1, k5, m1, k1 tbl) to end of round (96 sts).

Round 22: (M1, k6, m1, sl 1, k2 tog, psso, m1, k6, m1, k1 tbl) to end of round (108 sts).

Round 24: Kir, (sl 1, k1, psso, k4, m1, sl 1, k2 tog, psso, m1, k4, k2 tog, m1, k1, m1, k1 tbl, m1, k1, m1) to end of round (120 sts)

Round 26: (K5, m1, sl 1, k2 tog, psso, m1, k5, m1, k3, m1, k1 tbl, m1, k3, m1) to end of round (144 sts)

Round 28: (Sl 1, k1, psso, k3, m1, sl 1, k2 tog, psso, m1, k3, k2 tog, m1, k4, m1, k3, m1, k4, m1) to end of round (156 sts).

Round 30: (K4, m1, sl 1, k2 tog, psso, m1, k4, m1, sl 1, k1, psso, k3, m1, k5, m1, k3, k2 tog, m1) to end of round (168 sts).

Round 32: [Sl 1, k1, psso, k2, m1, sl 1, k2 tog, psso, m1, k2, k2 tog, (m1, sl 1, k1, psso, k3) twice, k2 tog, m1, k3, k2 tog, m1] to end of round (156 sts).

Round 34: [K3, m1, sl 1, k2 tog, psso, m1, k3, (m1, sl 1, k1, psso, k3) twice, k2 tog, m1, k3, k2 tog, m1] to end of round.

Round 36: [Sl 1, k1, psso, k1, m1, sl 1, k2 tog, psso, m1, k1, k2 tog, (m1, sl 1, k1, psso, k3) twice, k2 tog, m1, k3, k2 tog, m1] to end of round (144 sts).

Round 38: (Sl 1, k1, psso, m1, k3, m1, k2 tog, m1, sl 1, k2 tog, psso, k3, m1, k5, m1, k3, k3 tog, m1) to end of round.

Round 40: (M1, k1 tbl, m1, k2 tog, m1, k1 tbl, m1, sl 1, k1, psso, m1, k1 tbl, m1, sl 1, k2 tog, psso, k2, m1, k1 tbl, m1, sl 1, k1, psso, k1, k2 tog, m1, k1 tbl, m1, k2, k3 tog) to end of round (156 sts).

Round 42: [M1, k3, (m1, k1, m1, k3) twice, (m1, sl 1, k2 tog, psso, m1, k3) twice, m1, sl 1, k2 tog, psso] to end of round (180 sts).

Round 43: Knit.

Cast off in knitted picot.

Make another motif.

Cast off in plain knitting.

Make a lavender insert for the sachet.

When the two motifs are joined together, having one with a plain knitted cast-off gives a much neater finish. Insert the inner cushion. Close opening with fine stitches.

The sachet in the photograph has been decorated with tiny beads and an antique embroidered button.

LEAF

Materials

1 × 50 g ball DMC 20 cotton

Set of 4 double-pointed needles 2 mm (14)

Crochet hook 1.50 mm

White fabric for insert

Fibre filling

Lavender

Sewing needle and thread

Cast on 12 sts (4 sts on each of 3 needles). Work with 4th needle.

Rounds 1 and 2: Knit tbl.

Round 3: (M2, k2 tbl) to end of round (24 sts).

Round 4 and next two alternate Rounds: Knit tbl, working p1, k1, in each m2 of previous round

Round 5: K1 tbl to right, (m2, k4 tbl) to end of round (36 sts).

Round 7: K1 tbl to right, (m2, k6 tbl) to end of round (48 sts).

Round 9: K1 tbl to right, (m1, k4 tbl) to end of round (60 sts).

Round 10: K1 tbl. Knit into each m1 of previous round.

Round 11: (M1, k1, m1, k4 tbl) to end of round (84 sts).

Round 12: (K3, k4 tbl) to end of round.

Round 13: (M1, k3, m1, k2 tog tbl, k2 tbl, m1, k3, m1, k2 tbl, k2 tog tbl. Repeat to end of round (96 sts).

Round 14: (K5, k3 tbl) to end of round.

Round 15: (M1, k2 tog, k1, sl 1, k1, psso, m1, k2 tog tbl, k1 tbl, m1, k5, m1, k1 tbl, k2 tog tbl) to end of round.

Round 16: (K5, k2 tbl, k7, k2 tbl) to end of round.

Round 17: (M1, k2, knit twice in next st, k2, m1, k2 tog

tbl, m1, k7, m1, k2 tog tbl) to end of round (114 sts).

Round 18: (K8, k1 tbl, k9, k1 tbl) to end of round.

Round 19: (M1, k2, k2 tog, m2, sl 1, k1, psso, k2, m1, sl 1, k1, psso, k7, k2 tog) to end of round.

Round 20 and alternate Rounds: Knit, working p1, k1, into each m2 of previous round.

Round 21: (M1, k3, m2, sl 1, k1, psso, k2 tog, m2, k3, m1, sl 1, k1, psso, k5, k2 tog) to end of round (126 sts).

Round 23: [M1, k3, m2, (sl 1, k1, psso, k2 tog, m2) twice, k3, m1, sl 1, k1, psso, k3, k2 tog] to end of round (138 sts).

Round 25: [m1, k3, m2, (sl 1, k1, psso, k2 tog, m2) 3 times, k3, m1, sl 1, k1, psso, k1, k2 tog] to end of round (150 sts).

Round 27: [M1, k3, m2, (sl 1, k1, psso, k2 tog, m2) 4 times, k3, m1, sl 1, k2 tog, psso] to end of round (162 sts).

Round 28: K1 to right. Knit, working p1, k1 into each m2 of previous round.

Cast off thus:

Insert hook into 1st 4 sts. Pull cotton through 9ch, ★(1dc into next 4 sts, 9ch) 3 times, 1dc into next 3 sts, 9ch, (1dc into next 4 sts, 9ch) 3 times. Repeat from ★ omitting 1dc at end of last repeat; 1 sl st into 1st st. Fasten off.

To make up

Press the work under damp cloth. Pin out points, allow to dry. Make a circular insert approximately 14 cm (5½ inches) in diameter, lightly filled with fibre filling and lavender. Stitch the sachet together, enclosing the fabric insert.

DIAMOND

Materials

1 × 50 g ball DMC 20 cotton

Pair needles 1.75 mm (15)

Fine white fabric for sachet liner, 28 cm (11 inches)

Small piece of narrow silk ribbon (optional)

Sewing needle and thread

Press stud

Lavender and fibre filling

Measurements

Centre 9 cm × 10 cm (3½ inches × 4 inches)

Edging 4 cm (1½ inches) deep

Finished sachet approximately 18 cm (7 inches) in diameter

Centre

Cast on 22 sts.

Row 1: Sl 1, k2, (m1, k2 tog) 9 times, k1.

Row 2 and even Rows: M1, knit to end of row.

Row 3: M1, k9, k2 tog, m1, k1, m1, k2 tog, k9.

Row 5: M1, k2, (m1, k2 tog) 3 times, m1, k3 tog, m1, k3, (m1, k2 tog) 5 times, k1.

Row 7: M1, k9, k2 tog, m1, k5, m1, k2 tog, k9.

Row 9: M1, k2, (m1, k2 tog) 3 times, m1, k3 tog, m1, k2, k2 tog, m1, k3, (m1, k2 tog) 5 times, k1.

Row 11: M1, k9, k2 tog, m1, k2, k2 tog, m1, k1, m1, k2 tog, k2, m1, k2 tog, k9.

Radiating Circles *(instructions on page 33)*

Five Round Sachets. *Clockwise from bottom left:* **Star, Cyclamen, Leaf, Diamond and Victoria.** *(instructions on page 34)*

37

Lace Pomander and Four-Square Towel *(instructions on page 43)*

Crazy Patchwork Pillow *(instructions on page 45)*

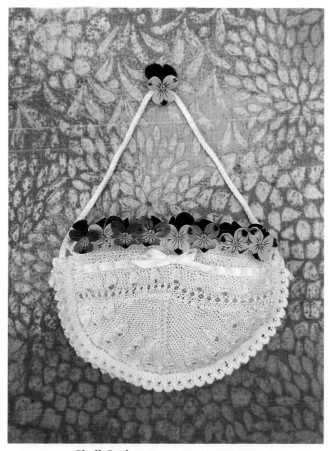

Shell Sachet *(instructions on page 47)*

Oval Hanging Sachet *(instructions on page 49)*

Web Sachet *(instructions on page 52)*

Three Square Sachets *(instructions on page 53)*

Ring Cushion *(instructions on page 56)*

40

Row 13: M1, k2, (m1, k2 tog) 3 times, m1, k3 tog, m1, k2, k2 tog, m1, k3, m1, k2 tog, k2, (m1, k2 tog) 5 times, k1.

Row 15: M1, k9, k2 tog, m1, k2, k2 tog, m1, k5, m1, k2 tog, k2, m1, k2 tog, k9.

Row 17: M1, k2, (m1, k2 tog) 3 times, m1, k3 tog, (m1, k2, k2 tog) twice, m1, k3, m1, k2 tog, k2, (m1, k2 tog) 5 times, k1.

Row 19: Sl 1, k8, k2 tog, (m1, k2, k2 tog) twice, m1, k1, (m1, k2 tog, k2) twice, m1, k2 tog, k9.

Row 21: Sl 1, k2, (m1, k2 tog) twice, m1, k3 tog, (m1, k2, k2 tog) twice, m1, k3, (m1, k2 tog, k2) twice, (m1, k2 tog) 4 times, k2.

Row 23: Sl 1, k6, k2 tog, (m1, k2, k2 tog) twice, m1, k5, (m1, k2 tog, k2) twice, m1, k2 tog, k7.

Row 25: Sl 1, k2, (m1, k2 tog) 4 times, (k2, m1, k2 tog) twice, k1, k2 tog, (m1, k2, k2 tog) twice, m1, k1, (m1, k2 tog) 3 times, k2.

Row 27: Sl 1, k9, (m1, k2 tog, k2) twice, m1, k3 tog, (m1, k2, k2 tog) twice, m1, k10.

Row 29: Sl 1, k2, (m1, k2 tog) 5 times, k2, m1, k2 tog, k5, k2 tog, m1, k2, k2 tog, m1, k1, (m1, k2 tog) 4 times, k2.

Row 31: Sl 1, k11, m1, k2 tog, k2, m1, k2 tog, k3, k2 tog, m1, k2, k2 tog, m1, k12.

Row 33: Sl 1, k2, (m1, k2 tog) 6 times, k2, m1, k2 tog, k1, k2 tog, m1, k2, k2 tog, m1, k1, (m1, k2 tog) 5 times, k2.

Row 35: Sl 1, k13, m1, k2 tog, k2, m1, k3 tog, m1, k2, k2 tog, m1, k14.

Row 37: Sl 1, k2, (m1, k2 tog) 7 times, k5, k2 tog, m1, k1, (m1, k2 tog) 6 times, k2.

Row 39: Sl 1, k15, m1, k2 tog, k3, k2 tog, m1, k16.

Row 41: Sl 1, k2, (m1, k2 tog) 8 times, k1, k2 tog, m1, k1, (m1, k2 tog) 7 times, k2.

Row 43: Sl 1, k17, m1, k3 tog, m1, k18.

Row 45: Sl 1, k2, (m1, k2 tog) 6 times, m1, k3 tog, m1, k3, (m1, k2 tog) 8 times, k2.

Row 47: Sl 1, k14, k2 tog, m1, k5, m1, k2 tog, k15.

Row 49: Sl 1, k2, (m1, k2 tog) 5 times, m1, k3 tog, m1, k2, k2 tog, m1, k3, (m1, k2 tog) 7 times, k2.

Row 51: Sl 1, k12, k2 tog, m1, k2, k2 tog, m1, k1, m1, k2 tog, k2, m1, k2 tog, k13.

Row 53: Sl 1, k2, (m1, k2 tog) 4 times, m1, k3 tog, m1, k2, k2 tog, m1, k3, m1, k2 tog, k2, (m1, k2 tog) 6 times, k2.

Row 55: Sl 1, k10, k2 tog, m1, k2, k2 tog, m1, k5, m1, k2 tog, k2, m1, k2 tog, k11.

Row 57: Sl 1, k2, (m1, k2 tog) 3 times, m1, k3 tog, (m1, k2, k2 tog) twice, m1, k3, m1, k2 tog, k2, (m1, k2 tog) 5 times, k2.

Row 59: As row 19.

Row 61: As row 21.

Row 63: As row 23.

Row 65: As row 25.

Row 67: As row 27.

Row 69: Sl 1, k2 tog, k2, (m1, k2 tog) 4 times, k2, m1, k2 tog, k5, k2 tog, m1, k2, k2 tog, m1, k1, (m1, k2 tog) 3 times, k1, k2 tog, k1.

Row 71: Sl 1, k2 tog, k8, m1, k2 tog, k2, m1, k2 tog, k3, k2 tog, m1, k2, k2 tog, m1, k8, k2 tog, k1.

Row 73: Sl 1, k2 tog, (m1, k2 tog) 5 times, k2, m1, k2 tog, k1, k2 tog, m1, k2, k2 tog, m1, k1, (m1, k2 tog) 4 times, k2 tog.

Row 75: Sl 1, k2 tog, k8, m1, k2 tog, k2, m1, k3 tog, m1, k2, k2 tog, m1, k8, k2 tog, k1.

Row 77: Sl 1, k2 tog, (m1, k2 tog) 5 times, k5, k2 tog, m1, k1, (m1, k2 tog) 4 times, k2 tog.

Row 79: Sl 1, k2 tog, k8, m1, k2 tog, k3, k2 tog, m1, k8, k2 tog, k1.

Row 81: Sl 1, k2 tog, (m1, k2 tog) 5 times, k1, k2 tog, m1, k1, (m1, k2 tog) 4 times, k2 tog.

Row 83: Sl 1, k2 tog, k8, m1, k3 tog, m1, k8, k2 tog, k1.

Cast off loosely.

Press lightly.

Lace edging

Cast on 16 sts.

Row 1: K10, (m1, k2 tog) twice, m1, k2.

Row 2: K10, p5. Turn.

Row 3: K9, (m1, k2 tog) twice, m1, k2.

Row 4: K11, p5. Turn.

Row 5: K10, (m1, k2 tog) twice, m1, k2.

Row 6: K12, p5. Turn.

Row 7: P5, k6, (m1, k2 tog) twice, m1, k2.

Row 8: Knit.

Row 9: K2, p5, k7, (m1, k2 tog) twice, m1, k2.

Row 10: K19. Turn.

Row 11: P5, k14.

Row 12: Cast off 5 sts, knit to end of row.

Repeat rows 1–12 until length desired.

Cast off.

Join ends of Diamond Lace edging and stitch around sachet centre. Make sachet liner and fill with lavender and fibre filling following basic instructions on page 13. Decorate with two ribbon bows, if desired.

VICTORIA

Materials

1 × 50 g ball DMC 20 cotton

Set of 4 double-pointed needles 2 mm (14)

(Make 2)

Cast on 8 sts (3 sts on each of 2 needles, 2 sts on 3rd needle). Knit with 4th needle.

Round 1: Knit.

Round 2: (M1, k1) to end of round (16 sts).

Knit 3 rounds.

Round 6: As round 2 (32 sts).

Knit 3 rounds.

Round 10: K1, (m1, k2) to last st, m1, k1 (48 sts).

Round 11: K1, (k1, p1, in each m1 of previous round, k2) to last 2 sts, k1, p1, into m1 of previous round, k1 (64 sts).

Round 12: (K2 tog, m1, sl 1, k1, psso) to end of round (48 sts).

Repeat rounds 11 and 12 four times

Round 21: K1, (k1, p1, k1, in each m1 of previous round, k2) to last 2 sts, k1, p1, k1, in m1 of previous round, k1 (80 sts).

Knit 3 rounds.

Round 25: (M1, k5) to end of round (96 sts).

Round 26 and alternate Rounds: Knit.

Round 27: (K1, m1, sl 1, k1, psso, k1, k2 tog, m1) to end of round.

Round 29: (M1, k2 tog, m1, sl 1, k2 tog, psso, m1, k1) to end of round.

Round 31: (Sl 1, k1, psso, m1) to end of round.

Round 33: (M1, k2 tog) to end of round.

Round 34: Knit.

Round 35: K1, (sl st from R.H. needle on to L.H. needle, insert needle into this st, cast on 2 sts, cast off 5 sts) until all sts have been cast off.

Cast off 2nd circle knitwise.

To make up

Press lightly. Make a small fabric circle filled with lavender and fibre filling to insert between the two knitted circles. Slip-stitch the circles neatly together. Knit a length of cord for bow and sew in place in the centre of the sachet.

13

Lace Pomander and Four-Square Towel

This delicate pomander in knitted lace, designed and knitted by the author, was embroidered by Joan Jackson. The deep edging gives a luxurious finish to the hand towel. Using a small needle size for the lace has produced a firm edging while retaining a delicate appearance. Lace by author.

Materials

• POMANDER

1 × 20 g ball DMC 20 cotton

Set of 4 double-pointed needles 2 mm (14)

Lavender

Fibre filling

DMC embroidery thread

Sewing needle and thread

• FOUR-SQUARE TOWEL EDGING

1 × 50 g ball DMC 10 cotton

Pair needles 1.25 mm (18)

Towel of size required

Sewing needle and thread for attaching edging

POMANDER

Cast on 2 sts on each of 3 needles. Work with 4th needle.

Round 1: Knit.

Round 2: (M1, k1) to end of round (12 sts).

Round 3: Knit.

Round 4: (M1, k2) to end of round.

Round 5: Knit.

Round 6: (M1, k3) to end of round.

Round 7: Knit.

Continue increasing in this manner until you have 22 sts on each needle. End with knit round.

Round 24: (M1, k4, sl 1, k2 tog, psso, k3, k in f & b of next st) to end of round.

Round 25: Knit.

Repeat rounds 24 and 25 eight times.

Cast off.

Embroider the lace pomander if desired. Fill with lavender and fibre filling and adjust filling to make a nicely rounded shape. Close the top by drawing the points together. Make a cord for the top, trim with tassel at the base. You might wish to use a coloured thread which tones with the embroidery for the cord and tassel.

FOUR-SQUARE TOWEL EDGING

Cast on 23 sts. Knit one row.

Row 1: Sl 1, k1, m1, k2 tog, k8, (m1, k2 tog) 5 times, m1, k1, (24 sts).

Row 2 and alternate Rows: M1, k2 tog, k to end of row.

Row 3: Sl 1, k1, m1, k2 tog, k9, (m1, k2 tog) 5 times, m1, k1 (25 sts).

Row 5: Sl 1, k1, m1, k2 tog, k10, (m1, k2 tog) 5 times, m1, k1 (26 sts).

Row 7: Sl 1, k1, m1, k2 tog, k11, (m1, k2 tog) 5 times, m1, k1 (27 sts).

Row 9: Sl 1, k1, m1, k2 tog, k12, (m1, k2 tog) 5 times, m1, k1 (28 sts).

Row 11: Sl 1, k1, m1, k2 tog, k6, m1, k2 tog, k5, (m1, k2 tog) 5 times, m1, k1 (29 sts).

Row 13: Sl 1, k1, m1, k2 tog, k5, (m1, k2 tog) twice, k5, (m1, k2 tog) 5 times, m1, k1 (30 sts).

Row 15: Sl 1, k1, m1, k2 tog, k4, (m1, k2 tog) 3 times, k5, (m1, k2 tog) 5 times, m1, k1 (31 sts).

Row 17: Sl 1, k1, m1, k2 tog, k3, (m1, k2 tog) 4 times, k5, (m1, k2 tog) 5 times, k1 (31 sts).

Row 19: Sl 1, k1, m1, k2 tog, k4, (m1, k2 tog) 3 times, k4, k2 tog, (m1, k2 tog) 5 times, k1 (30 sts).

Row 21: Sl 1, k1, m1, k2 tog, k5, (m1, k2 tog) twice, k4, k2 tog, (m1, k2 tog) 5 times, k1 (29 sts).

Row 23: Sl 1, k1, m1, k2 tog, k6, m1, k2 tog, k4, k2 tog, (m1, k2 tog) 5 times, k1 (28 sts).

Row 25: Sl 1, k1, m1, k2 tog, k11, k2 tog, (m1, k2 tog) 5 times, k1 (27 sts).

Row 27: Sl 1, k1, m1, k2 tog, k10, k2 tog, (m1, k2 tog) 5 times, k1 (26 sts).

Row 29: Sl 1, k1, m1, k2 tog, k9, k2 tog, (m1, k2 tog) 5 times, k1 (25 sts).

Row 31: Sl 1, k1, m1, k2 tog, k8, k2 tog, (m1, k2 tog) 5 times, k1 (24 sts).

Row 33: Sl 1, k1, m1, k2 tog, k7, k2 tog, (m1, k2 tog) 5 times, k1 (23 sts).

Row 35: Sl 1, k1, (m1, k2 tog) 10 times, k1 (23 sts).

Row 36: As row 2.

Repeat rows 1–36 until length desired.

Cast off.

Press the lace and attach to the towel with tiny firm stitches.

14

Crazy Patchwork Pillow

A crazy patchwork pillow in silk dupion. Joan has collected choice pieces of fabric and lace motifs for the patchwork. The clever use of knitted lace enhances the design. Pillow designed and made by Joan Eckersley.

Materials

Quantity of materials for crazy patchwork

Sewing needle and thread

Lavender insert

- PATTERN 1
1 × 10 g ball DMC 12 cotton, blanc neige
Pair needles 1.25 mm (18)

- PATTERN 2
1 × 20 g ball DMC 40 cotton
Pair needles 1.50 mm (16)

- PATTERN 3
2 × 20 g balls DMC 40 cotton
Pair needles 1.50 mm (16)

- PATTERN 4
1 × 20 g ball DMC 40 cotton
Pair needles 1.50 mm (16)

- PATTERN 5
1 × 20 g ball DMC Cébélia 20 cotton
Pair needles 1.75 mm (15)

- PATTERN 6
1 × 20 g ball DMC 40 cotton
Pair needles 1.25 mm (18)

PATTERN 1
(bottom left hand corner of pillow)

Cast on 13 sts. Knit one row.

Row 1: Sl 1, k3, m1, k5, m1, k2 tog, m1, k2 (15 sts).

Row 2: K2, p11, k2.

Row 3: Sl 1, k4, sl 1, k2 tog, psso, k2, (m1, k2 tog) twice, k1 (13 sts).

Row 4: K2, p9, k2.

Row 5: Sl 1, k3, sl 1, k1, psso, k2, (m1, k2 tog) twice, k1 (12 sts).

Row 6: K2, p8, k2.

Row 7: Sl 1, k2, sl 1, k1, psso, k2, (m1, k2 tog) twice, k1 (11 sts).

Row 8: K2, p7, k2.

Row 9: Sl 1, k1, sl 1, k1, psso, k2, (m1, k2 tog) twice, k1 (10 sts).

Row 10: K2, p6, k2.

Row 11: Sl 1, sl 1, k1, psso, k2, m1, k1, m1, k2 tog, m1, k2 (11 sts).

Row 12: K2, p7, k2.

Row 13: Sl 1, k3, m1, k3, m1, k2 tog, m1, k2 (13 sts).

Row 14: K2, p9, k2.

Repeat rows 1–14 until length desired.

PATTERN 2
(left hand edging near butterfly)

Cast on 7 sts. Knit one row.

Row 1: Sl 1, k2, m1, k2 tog, m2, k2.

Row 2: K3, p1, k2, m1, k2 tog, k1.

Row 3: Sl 1, k2, m1, k2 tog, k4.

Row 4: Cast off 2 sts. K3, m1, k2 tog, k1.

Repeat rows 1–4 until length desired.

PATTERN 3
(central medallion)

NB Two balls of cotton are required for this pattern.

Cast on 8 sts. Knit one row.

Join 2nd ball of thread to 1st st, knotting it to hold it firm. The knot can be undone and the ends woven through on completion.

Using original thread work thus:

Row 1: Sl 1, k2. Bring 2nd thread across in front and place between needles. Proceed using this thread.

Row 2: Sl 1, k2, m2, k2.

Row 3: K3, p1, k3. Turn.

Row 4: Sl 1, k1, m1, k2 tog, k3.

Row 5: Cast off 2 sts, k4. Turn.

Continue knitting pattern from rows 2–5, working 5 patterns in all. Pick up other thread. Knit as follows the 3 sts remaining on L.H. needle

Row 6: K3.

Row 7: Sl 1, k2. Turn.

Continue rows 6–7, working 7 patterns in all, then sl 1, k3. Turn.

Knit 4.

Continue from row 1 until length desired.

NB Rows 6–7 can be worked more or less times depending on how much you require to shape the edge. Cast off. Join ends of edging neatly.

PATTERN 4
(lower right)

Cast on 49 sts. Knit one row.

Row 1: K1, (m1, sl 1, k1, psso, k7, k2 tog, m1, k1) to end of row.

Row 2 and alternate Rows: K1, p47, k1 (49 sts).

Row 3: K2, m1, sl 1, k1, psso, k5, (k2 tog, m1, k3, m1, sl 1, k1, psso, k5) to last 4 sts, k2 tog, m1, k2.

Row 5: K3, m1, sl 1, k1, psso, k3, (k2 tog, m1, k5, m1, sl 1, k1, psso, k3) to last 5 sts, k2 tog, m1, k3.

Row 7: (K1, k2 tog, m1, k1, m1, sl 1, k1, psso) to last st, k1.

Row 9: K2 tog, m1, k3, (m1, sl 1, k2 tog, psso, m1, k3) to last 2 sts, m1, sl 1, k1, psso.

Row 11: K4, k2 tog, m1, k1, m1, sl 1, k1, psso, (k7, k2 tog, m1, k1, m1, sl 1, k1, psso) to last 4 sts, k4.

Row 13: K3, k2 tog, m1, k3, m1, sl 1, k1, psso, (k5, k2 tog, m1, k3, m1, sl 1, k1, psso) to last 3 sts, k3.

Row 15: K2, k2 tog, m1, k5, m1, sl 1, k1, psso, (k3, k2 tog, m1, k5, m1, sl 1, k1, psso) to last 2 sts, k2.

Row 17: (K1, k2 tog, m1, k1, m1, sl 1, k1, psso) to last st, k1.

Row 19: K2 tog, m1, k3, (m1, sl 1, k2 tog, psso, m1, k3) to last 2 sts, m1, sl 1, k1, psso.

Row 20: Purl. (Knit 1st and last st.)

Repeat rows 1–20 until length desired.

PATTERN 5
(upper right, near medallion)

Cast on 44 sts.

Row 1: Knit.

Row 2: Purl.

Row 3: K2, (m1, p1, p3 tog, p1, m1, k2) to end of row.

Row 4: Purl.

Repeat rows 1–4 until length required.

PATTERN 6
(lower right, near Row edging)

Cast on 4 sts. Knit one row.

Row 1: K1, p3

Row 2: K1, m1, k1 tbl, m1, sl 1, k1, psso.

Row 3: K1, p2, (k1, p1, k1, p) into next st, p1.

Row 4: Cast off 4 sts. K1, m1, sl 1, k1, psso (4 sts).

Repeat rows 1-4 until length desired.

To make up

See any basic patchwork book for instructions on assembling crazy patchwork,

15

Shell Sachet

This charming shell-shaped sachet can be hung in your wardrobe, or on a wall to perfume the air. Designed and made by Ruth Rintoule, it is based on an old pattern from the white knitted bedspread era. Hung on the finial of a dressing-table mirror, this type of sachet was popularly used as a hair receiver (that is, to hold the hair pads known as 'rats' used to pad out bouffant hair styles).

Materials

1 × 50 g ball DMC 20 cotton

2 pairs needles, 3 mm (11) and 1.75 mm (15)

1 m (40 inches) white ribbon

Small piece cotton fabric

Press stud

Sewing needle and thread

Body of sachet

Use 3 mm (11) needles.

(make 2)

Cast on 66 sts

Row 1: (Wrong side) knit.

Row 2: P2 tog, p4, (*pick up the thread lying between st just worked and the next one, knit into it 5 times*, p6) 9 times. Repeat *—*, p4, p2 tog.

Row 3: K5, (p5, k6) 9 times, p5, k5.

Row 4: P2 tog, p3, (sl 1, k1, psso, k1, k2 tog, p6) 9 times, sl 1, k1, psso, k1, k2 tog, p3, p2 tog.

Row 5: K4, (p3, k6) 9 times, p3, k4.

Row 6: P2 tog, p2, (sl 1, k2 tog, psso, p6) 9 times, sl 1, k2 tog, psso, p2, p2 tog.

Row 7: K2, (k2 tog, k5) 9 times, k2 tog, k3.

Rows 8–12: Repeat rows 2–6 with one triangular motif less.

Row 13: K2, (k2 tog, k5) 4 times, k7, (k2 tog, k5) 3 times, k2 tog, k3.

Row 14: P2 tog, p4, ** (pick up the thread between st just worked and the next st, knit into it 5 times, p6) **, p9, k1, p9. Repeat **—**, p4, p2 tog.

Row 15–19: Continue the 3 motifs placed at each side of centre, beginning and ending every other row with p2 tog. Also p2 tog before and after the centre st. Always knit the centre st on right side and wrong side of work until the semi-circle is completed.

Row 20: Work in st st, beginning and ending every other row with k2 tog. On centre 5 sts, k2 tog, k1, sl 1, k1, psso when 3 sts remain.

Cast off.

Top of semi-circle

Pick up 58 sts along top of semi-circle.

Row 1: Purl.

Row 2: Knit.

Row 3: Purl.

Row 4: ★k2 tog, m1★. Repeat ★—★ to end.

Row 5: Purl.

Rows 6 and 7: Knit.

Row 8: P4, ★★(pick up the thread lying between st just worked and the next st, knit into it 5 times, p6)★★. Repeat ★★—★★ (this starts a line of triangular motifs).

Rows 9–13: Continue straight, forming motifs as in rows 3–7 of instructions for semi-circle

Row 14: Knit.

Row 15: Purl.

Row 16: ★k2 tog, m1★. Repeat ★—★ to end.

Row 17: Purl.

Row 18: Knit.

Row 19: Purl.

Cast off.

Edging

(Make 2 pieces of edging to go around sachet, and 1 piece to go around top.) Use 1.75 mm (15) needles.

Cast on 5 sts.

Row 1: Knit.

Row 2: K2, m1, k3.

Row 3: K4, m1, k2.

Row 4: K3, m1, k4.

Row 5: K5, m1, k3.

Row 6: Cast off 4 sts. Knit 5.

Repeat rows 1–6 until length required.

Cast off.

To make up

Stitch lace to both edges, join edges together. Stitch around top. Thread ribbon through holes at top, making a bow at front and back of sachet. Attach a length of ribbon or knitted cord to hang sachet. Sew on press stud. Insert semi-circular lavender sachet.

16

Oval Hanging Sachet

A distinctively shaped tasselled sachet from the nineteenth century, expertly replicated by Ruth Rintoule.

Materials

1 × 50 g ball DMC 20 cotton
Pair needles 1.25 mm (18)
Small button
Sewing thread and needle
Lavender and fibre filling
Small piece of fine white fabric for lavender insert

Sachet

Cast on 3 sts, m1, k3, increase in this manner until you have 10 sts on the needle.

Row 1: M1, k3, k2 tog, m1, k5.

Row 2 and alternate Rows: M1, knit to end of row.

Row 3: M1, k3, k2 tog, m1, k1, m1, k2 tog, k4.

Row 5: M1, k3, k2 tog, m1, k3, m1, k2 tog, k4.

Row 7: M1, k3, k2 tog, m1, k5, m1, k2 tog, k4.

Row 9: M1, k3, k2 tog, m1, k3, m1, k1, m1, k3, m1, k2 tog, k4.

Row 11: M1, k3, k2 tog, m1, k2, k2 tog, m1, k3, m1, k2 tog, k2, m1, k2 tog, k4.

Row 13: M1, k3, k2 tog, m1, k2, k2 tog, m1, k5, m1, k2 tog, k2, m1, k2 tog, k4.

Row 15: M1, k3, k2 tog, m1, k2, k2 tog, m1, k7, m1, k2 tog, k2, m1, k2 tog, k4.

Row 17: M1, k3, k2 tog, m1, k2, k2 tog, m1, k3, k2 tog, m2, k4, m1, k2 tog, k2, m1, k2 tog, k4.

Row 18: M1, k14, (k1, p1) in m2 of previous row, k14.

Row 19: M1, k3, k2 tog, (m1, k2, k2 tog) twice, m2, (k2 tog) twice, m2, k2 tog, k2, m1, k2 tog, k2, m1, k2 tog, k4.

Row 20 and alternate Rows: M1, knit, (k1, p1) in each m2 of previous row.

Row 21: M1, k3, k2 tog, m1, k2, k2 tog, m1, k5, k2 tog, m2, k2 tog, k5, m1, k2 tog, k2, m1, k2 tog, k4.

Row 23: M1, k3, k2 tog, m1, k2, k2 tog, m1, k4, k2 tog, m2, (k2 tog) twice, k2, k2 tog, k4, m1, k2 tog, k2, m1, k2 tog, k4

Row 25: M1, k3, k2 tog, m1, k2, k2 tog, m1, k7, k2 tog, m2, k2 tog, k7, m1, k2 tog, k2, m1, k2 tog, k4.

Row 27: M1, k3, k2 tog, m1, k2, k2 tog, m1, k20, m1, k2 tog, k2, m1, k2 tog, k4.

Row 29: M1, k3, k2 tog, m1, k2, k2 tog, m1, k4, k2 tog, m2, k2 tog, k6, k2 tog, m2, k2 tog, k4, m1, k2 tog, k2, m1, k2 tog, k4.

Row 31: M1, k3, k2 tog, m1, k2, k2 tog, m1, k3, k2 tog, m2, (k2 tog) twice, m2, k2 tog, k2, k2 tog, m2, (k2 tog) twice, m2, k2 tog, k3, m1, k2 tog, k2, m1, k2 tog, k4.

Row 33: M1, k3, k2 tog, m1, k2, k2 tog, m1, k6, k2 tog, m2, k2 tog, k6, k2 tog, m2, k2 tog, k6, m1, k2 tog, k2, m1, k2 tog, k4.

Row 35: M1, k3, k2 tog, m1, k2, k2 tog, m1, k5, k2 tog, m2, (k2 tog) twice, m2, k2 tog, k2, k2 tog, m2, (k2 tog) twice, m2, k2 tog, k5, m1, k2 tog, k2, m1, k2 tog, k4.

Row 37: M1, k3, k2 tog, m1, k2, k2 tog, m1, k8, k2 tog, m2, k2 tog, k6, k2 tog, m2, k2 tog, k8, m1, k2 tog, k2, m1, k2 tog, k4.

Row 38 and alternate Rows: M1, k2 tog, (k1, p1) in each m2 of previous row.

Row 39: M1, k2 tog, k1, k2 tog, m1, k2, k2 tog, m1, k32, m1, k2 tog, k2, m1, k2 tog, k3.

Row 41: M1, k2 tog, k1, k2 tog, m1, k2, k2 tog, m1, k4, k2 tog, m2, k2 tog, (k6, k2 tog, m2, k2 tog) twice, k4, m1, k2 tog, k2, m1, k2 tog, k3.

Row 43: M1, k2 tog, k1, (k2 tog, m1, k2) twice, k2 tog, m2, (k2 tog) twice, m2, k2 tog, k2, k2 tog, m2, (k2 tog) twice, m2, k2 tog, k2, k2 tog, m2, (k2 tog) twice, m2, k2 tog, (k3, m1, k2 tog) twice, k3.

Row 45: M1, k2 tog, k1, k2 tog, m1, k2, k2 tog, m1, k4, k2 tog, m2, k2 tog, (k6, k2 tog, m2, k2 tog) twice, k4, m1, k2 tog, k2, m1, k2 tog, k3.

Row 47: As row 43.

Row 49: As row 45.

Row 51: M1, k2 tog, k1, k2 tog, m1, k2, k2 tog, m1, k32, m1, k2 tog, k2, m1, k2 tog, k3.

Row 53: M1, k2 tog, k1, k2 tog, m1, k2, k2 tog, m1, k9, k2 tog, m2, k2 tog, k6, k2 tog, m2, k2 tog, k9, m1, k2 tog, k2, m1, k2 tog, k3.

Row 55: M1, k2 tog, k1, k2 tog, m1, k2, k2 tog, m1, k7, k2 tog, m2, (k2 tog) twice, m2, k2 tog, k2, k2 tog, m2, (k2 tog) twice, m2, k2 tog, k7, m1, k2 tog, k2, m1, k2 tog, k3.

Row 57: As row 53.

Row 59: As row 55.

Row 61: As row 53.

Row 63: As row 51.

Row 65: M1, k2 tog, k1, k2 tog, m1, k2, k2 tog, m1, k14, k2 tog, m2, k2 tog, k14, m1, k2 tog, k2, m1, k2 tog, k3.

Row 67: M1, k2 tog, k1, k2 tog, m1, k2, k2 tog, m1, k12, k2 tog, m2, (k2 tog) twice, m2, k2 tog, k12, m1, k2 tog, k2, m1, k2 tog, k3.

Row 69: As row 65.

Row 71: As row 67.

Row 73: As row 65.

Row 75: As row 51.

Row 77: As row 53.

Row 79: As row 55.

Row 81: As row 53.

Row 83: As row 55.

Row 85: As row 53.

Row 87: As row 51.

Row 89: As row 41.

Row 91: As row 43.

Row 93: As row 45.

Row 95: As row 43.

Row 97: As row 41.

Row 99: As row 51.

Decrease thus:

Row 101: M1, k2 tog, k1, k2 tog, m1, k2, k2 tog, m1, k2 tog, k7, k2 tog, m2, k2 tog, k6, k2 tog, m2, k2 tog, k7, k2 tog, m1, k2 tog, k2, m1, k2 tog, k3.

Row 102 and alternate Rows: M1, k2 tog, knit, working k1, p1, in each m2 of previous row.

Row 103: M1, k2 tog, k1, k2 tog, m1, k2, k2 tog, m1, k2 tog, k4, k2 tog, m2, (k2 tog) twice, m2, k2 tog, k2, k2 tog, m2, (k2 tog) twice, m2, k2 tog, k4, k2 tog, m1, k2 tog, k2, m1, k2 tog, k3.

Row 105: M1, k2 tog, k1, k2 tog, m1, k2, k2 tog, m1, k2 tog, k5, k2 tog, m2, k2 tog, k6, k2 tog, m2, k2 tog, k5, k2 tog, m1, k2 tog, k2, m1, k2 tog, k3.

Row 107: M1, k2 tog, k1, k2 tog, m1, k2, k2 tog, m1, k2 tog, k2, k2 tog, m2, (k2 tog) twice, m2, k2 tog, k2, k2 tog, m2, (k2 tog) twice, m2, k2 tog, k2, k2 tog, m1, k2 tog, k2, m1, k2 tog, k3.

Row 109: M1, k2 tog, k1, k2 tog, m1, k2, k2 tog, m1, k2 tog, k3, k2 tog, m2, k2 tog, k6, k2 tog, m2, k2 tog, k3, k2 tog, m1, k2 tog, k2, m1, k2 tog, k3.

Row 111: M1, k2 tog, k1, k2 tog, m1, k2, k2 tog, m1, k2 tog, k18, k2 tog, m1, k2 tog, k2, m1, k2 tog, k3.

Row 113: M1, k2 tog, k1, k2 tog, m1, k2, k2 tog, m1, k2 tog, k6, k2 tog, m2, k2 tog, k6, k2 tog, m1, k2 tog, k2, m1, k2 tog, k3.

Row 115: M1, k2 tog, k1, k2 tog, m1, k2, k2 tog, m1, k2 tog, k3, k2 tog, m2, (k2 tog) twice, m2, k2 tog, k3, k2 tog, m1, k2 tog, k2, m1, k2 tog, k3.

Row 117: M1, k2 tog, k1, k2 tog, m1, k2, k2 tog, m1, k2 tog, k4, k2 tog, m2, k2 tog, k4, k2 tog, m1, k2 tog, k2, m1, k2 tog, k3.

Row 119: M1, k2 tog, k1, k2 tog, m1, k2, k2 tog, m1, k2 tog, k1, k2 tog, m2, (k2 tog) twice, m2, k2 tog, k1, k2 tog, m1, k2 tog, k2, m1, k2 tog, k3.

Row 121: M1, k2 tog, k1, k2 tog, m1, k2, k2 tog, m1, k2 tog, k2, k2 tog, m2, k2 tog, k2, k2 tog, m1, k2 tog, k2, m1, k2 tog, k3.

Row 123: M1, k2 tog, k1, k2 tog, m1, k2, k2 tog, m1, k2 tog, k6, k2 tog, m1, k2 tog, k2, m1, k2 tog, k3.

Row 125: M1, k2 tog, k1, k2 tog, m1, k2, k2 tog, m1, k2 tog, k4, k2 tog, m1, k2 tog, k2, m2, k2 tog, k3.

Row 127: M1, k2 tog, k1, k2 tog, m1, k2, k2 tog, m1, k2 tog, k2, k2 tog, m1, k2 tog, k2, m1, k2 tog, k3.

Row 129: M1, k2 tog, k1, k2 tog, m1, k2, k2 tog, m1, (k2 tog) twice, m1, k2 tog, k2, m1, k2 tog, k3.

Row 131: M1, k2 tog, k1, k2 tog, m1, k2, k2 tog, (m1, k2 tog) twice, k2, m1, k2 tog, k3.

Row 133: M1, k2 tog, k1, k2 tog, m1, k2, k2 tog, k1, k2 tog, k2, m1, k2 tog, k3.

Row 135: M1, k2 tog, k1, k2 tog, m1, k2, sl 1, k2 tog, psso, k2, m1, k2 tog, k3.

Row 137: M1, k2 tog, k1, k2 tog, m1, k1, sl 1, k2 tog, psso, k1, m1, k2 tog, k3.

Row 139: M1, k2 tog, k1, k2 tog, m1, sl 1, k2 tog, psso, m1, k2 tog, k3.

Row 141: M1, k2 tog, (k1, k2 tog) twice, k3.

Row 143: M1, k2 tog, k1, sl 1, k2 tog, psso, k3.

Row 145: M1, k2 tog, sl 1, k2 tog, psso, k2.

Row 146: (K2 tog) twice, k1.

Row 147: Sl 1, k2 tog, psso.

Break thread. Draw through remaining sts.

Fasten off.

Repeat rows 1–147 for back of sachet.

Edging

Cast on 10 sts.

Row 1: (M1, k2 tog) 4 times, m1, k2.

Row 2 and alternate Rows: Knit, working k1, p1, in made sts of previous row.

Row 3: Sl 1, k8, m1, k2.

Row 5: Sl 1, k9, m1, k2.

Row 7: Sl 1, k3, k2 tog, m2, k2 tog, k3, m1, k2.

Row 9: Sl 1, k1, (k2 tog, m2, k2 tog) twice, k2, m1, k2.

Row 11: Sl 1, k3, k2 tog, m2, k2 tog, k5, m1, k2.

Row 13: Sl 1, k1, (k2 tog, m2, k2 tog) twice, k1, k2 tog, m1, k2 tog, k1.

Row 15: Sl 1, k3, k2 tog, m2, (k2 tog) 3 times, m1, k2 tog, k1.

Row 17: Sl 1, k5, (k2 tog) twice, m1, k2 tog, k1.

Row 19: Sl 1, k5, k2 tog, m1, k2 tog, k1.

Row 20: Knit.

Repeat rows 1–20 until length desired.

To make up

Press the two centres lightly. Join, leaving an opening for lavender insert and filling. Stitch the border around sachet. Make a tassel for the bottom. Use ribbon or a covered ring to hang the sachet. Close sachet with button and loop or slip-stitch opening.

17

Web Sachet

A beautiful sachet in the Web design, with fluted edging. Designed and knitted by Ruth Rintoule based on old patterns c.1890s.

Materials

1 × 20 g ball DMC 20 cotton

Set of 5 needles, 1.75 mm (16)

Button

Hexagonal taffeta sachet and internal organza sachet (see page 13)

Press stud

Sewing needle and thread

Fibre filling and lavender

Web pattern

Cast on 240 sts (60 sts on each of 4 needles). Work with 5th needle.

Knit 2 rounds.

Round 1: (K2, p2 tog, p34, p2 tog) to end of round.

Round 2: (K2, p36) to end of round.

Round 3: As round 2.

Round 4: (K2, p2 tog, p32, p2 tog) to end of round.

Rounds 5 and 6: (K2 tog, p34) to end of round.

Round 7: (K2, k2 tog, k30, sl 1, k1, psso) to end of round.

Rounds 8 and 9: Knit.

Round 10: (K2, k2 tog, k28, sl 1, k1, psso) to end of round.

Rounds 11 and 12: Knit.

Continue in pattern, working 6 rounds purl, 6 rounds knit, and keeping the 2 knit sts as set until 24 sts remain.

Continue thus:

Round 1: (K2, k2 tog) to end of round.

Round 2: (K2 tog, k1) to end of round.

Break off thread. Draw through sts.

Fluted edging

Cast on 12 sts.

Row 1: Knit.

Row 2: Sl 1, knit to end of row.

Row 3: Purl.

Row 4: Sl 1, purl to end of row.

Repeat rows 1–4 until length required, allowing enough length to ease the edging around the points of the Web.

Cast off.

Join ends of edging and attach to Web centre. Do not press the work.

To make up

Fit knitting over hexagonal taffeta sachet and stitch to edges of sachet between centre and lace edging. Slip organza insert inside and close up with tiny stitches. Sew a button in the centre if you wish.

18

Three Square Sachets

(Pictured page 40.) Eight-Pointed Star on the left was adapted by Edna Lomas from a motif for an early bedspread pattern to make a square sachet. The two motifs are thonged with ribbon, eliminating the need for sewing and enabling you to match the décor of the recipient of your gift. White Rose, in the centre, designed by the author and knitted by Edna Lomas, is made from two large motifs from the white bedspread era. Again, joining the two motifs with coloured silk ribbon enables you to match a particular decorative scheme, and allows for easy removal of the insert for replenishing and of the sachet cover for laundering. Cross-Stitch on the right is an incredible piece of work from master knitter Ruth Rintoule, using fine yarn and tiny needles to create a sachet approximately 9 cm (3½ inches) square with a wide lace edging.

EIGHT-POINTED STAR

Materials

1 × 50 g ball DMC 20 cotton

Set of 5 double-pointed needles 2 mm (14)

1 metre (40 inches) of narrow silk ribbon

Basic lavender sachet 15 cm (6 inches) square

(make 2)

Cast on 8 sts (2 sts on each of 4 needles). Work with 5th needle.

Round 1 and alternate Rounds: Knit.

Round 2: (M1, k1) to end of round.

Repeat these 2 rounds twice (64 sts).

Mark beginning of round:

Round 8: (M1, k8) to end of round (72 sts).

Round 10: (M1, k1, m1, k6, k2 tog) to end of round (80 sts).

Round 12: (M1, k3, m1, k5, k2 tog) to end of round (88 sts).

Round 14: (M1, sl 1, k1, psso, k1, k2 tog, m1, k4, k2 tog) to end of round (80 sts).

Round 16: (M1, k1, m1, sl 1, k2 tog, psso, m1, k1, m1, k3, k2 tog) to end of round (88 sts).

Round 18: (M1, k3, m1, k1, m1, k3, m1, k2, k2 tog) to end of round (112 sts).

Round 20: (M1, sl 1, k1, psso, k1, k2 tog, m1, k1, m1, sl 1, k1, psso, k1, k2 tog, m1, k1, k2 tog) to end of round (104 sts).

Round 22: (M1, k1, m1, sl 1, k2 tog, psso, m1, k3, m1, sl 1, k2 tog, psso, m1, k1, m1, k2 tog) to end of round.

Round 24: (M1, k3, m1, k1, m1, sl 1, k1, psso, k1, k2 tog, m1, k1, m1, k3, m1, k1) to end of round (144 sts).

Round 26: (M1, sl 1, k1, psso, k1, k2 tog, m1, k2, m1, sl 1, k2 tog, psso, m1, k2, m1, sl 1, k1, psso, k1, k2 tog, m1, k1) to end of round (144 sts).

Round 28: M1, k1, ★(m1, sl 1, k2 tog, psso, m1, k4, m1, k1, m1, k4, m1, sl 1, k2 tog, psso)★, m1, k3, then repeat from ★—★ once, (m1, k1) twice. Repeat from beginning of round on each needle (168 sts).

Round 30: (M1, p41, m1, k1) to end of round (176 sts).

Round 32: As round 30 (184 sts).

Round 34: [M1, k1, (m1, k2 tog) ?? times, m1, k1]. Repeat to end (192 sts).

Round 36: As round 30 (200 sts).

Round 37: Knit.

Cast off knitwise.

To make up

Dampen and pin out each motif to a square. Insert lavender square before closing fourth side. With a bodkin, thread the ribbon through the holes in the four sides of motif, tying a small bow at each corner.

WHITE ROSE

Materials

2 × 50 g balls DMC 10 cotton

Pair needles 2 mm (14)

Cushion for insert

Small amount of green ribbon

1 ball DMC Perle 8 cotton

4 rose design buttons

Sewing needle and thread

Cast on 1 st.

Row 1: K1, p1, k1 into st.

Row 2: Knit.

Row 3: Purl twice into 1st st, p1. Purl twice into last st.

Row 4: Knit.

Row 5: Knit twice into 1st st, k to last st. Knit twice into last st.

Row 6: Purl.

Row 7: As row 5.

Row 8: Knit.

Row 9: Purl twice into 1st st, p to last st. Purl twice into last st.

Row 10: Knit.

Row 11: As row 5.

Row 12: (P2 tog) to last st, p1.

Row 13: Knit twice into 1st st, (m1, k1) to last st, m1. Knit twice in last st.

Rows 14 to 18: As rows 6 to 10.

Rows 19 to 27: As rows 5 to 13 (29 sts).

Repeat last 14 rows (43 sts).

Rows 42 to 46: As rows 6 to 10.

Rows 47 to 50: As rows 5 to 8.

Row 51: Purl twice into 1st st (m1, p2 tog, p4) 8 times, m1, p2 (53 sts).

Row 52: K2, [(k1, p1) 3 times in next st, k5] 8 times, (k1, p1) 3 times in next st, k2.

Row 53: Purl twice into 1st st, p1, (k6, p5) 8 times, k6, p1. Purl twice into last st.

Row 54: K3, (p2 tog, p2, p2 tog tbl, k5) 8 times, p2 tog, p2, p2 tog tbl, k3.

Row 55: Purl twice into 1st st, p2, (k4, p5) 8 times, k4, p2. Purl twice into last st.

Row 56: K4, (p2 tog, p2 tog tbl, k5) 8 times, p2 tog, p2 tog tbl, k4.

Row 57: Purl twice into 1st st, p3, (k2, k5) 8 times, k2, p3. Purl twice into last st.

Row 58: (K5, p2 tog tbl) 9 times, k5.

Row 59: Purl twice into 1st st, p1, (m1, p2 tog, p1, k1, p2) 9 times, m1, p2 tog. Purl twice into last st.

Row 60: K3, [(k1, p1) 3 times in next st, k5] 9 times, (k1, p1) 3 times in next st, k3.

Row 61: P3, (k6, p5) 9 times, k6, p3.

Rows 62 to 65: As rows 54 to 57, having 9 repeats instead of 8.

Rows 66 to 69: As rows 58 to 61, having 10 repeats.

Rows 70 to 73: As rows 54 to 57, working extra repeats.

Row 74: As row 58, working extra repeats.

Rows 75 to 80: As rows 11 to 16.

Cast off.

Make three more triangles in the same way. Lightly press and sew neatly together to form square.

Make back of sachet the same as front. Back and front are held together by threading narrow ribbon through the holes. The sachet illustrated has a white rose button attached to each corner of the inner square and a knitted white rose in the centre square. Finely knitted cord looped around the rose adds a touch of colour.

Knitted rose

Cast on 2 sts.

First layer:

Row 1: M1, k to end.

Row 2: Sl 1, k to end.

Repeat rows 1 and 2 until there are 9 sts on needle, ending with row 2.

Row 3: M1, k3 tog, k to end.

Row 4: Sl 1, k to end.

Repeat from row 1 until 9 petals have been worked.

Cast off.

Second layer

Work as first layer until petal has 7 sts. Decrease until 2 sts remain.

Make 9 petals.

Cast off.

Third layer

Work as first layer until petal has 5 sts. Make 5 petals.

Cast off.

Thread yarn through straight edge and draw up to form circle. Stitch layers together to form flower. Add lengths of knitted cord to frame flower.

Using double-pointed needles, make knitted cord thus:

Cast on 3 sts.

Row 1: (K3, do not turn, slide to other end of needle). Repeat until length desired.

CROSS-STITCH

Materials

1 × 50 g ball DMC 40 cotton

Pair double-pointed needles 1.25 mm (18)

Fine white fabric, approx. 40 cm (16 inches)

Organza or net for lavender insert

Sewing needle and thread

1 metre (40 inches) narrow ribbon

Lavender and fibre filling

Centre

NB This pattern can be a little tricky. Please follow with care.

Cast on 44 sts.

Rows 1 and 2: Knit.

Row 3: Sl 1, k1, turn. Knit the 2 sts again, then knit again. Begin the cross st thus: sl 1, k1, *pass the thread around needle 3 times and k1. Repeat from * to last 2 sts, k2.

Row 4: Sl 1, k1, turn. Knit the 2 sts again. Begin the cross st thus: sl 1, k1. *Insert needle in next st purlwise. Slip the st unworked onto R.H. needle and at the same time drop the twisted thread from L.H. needle and absorb it by drawing it into the stitch just slipped, letting the thread into a long loose stitch*. Repeat *—* until all twisted sts are used and you have the whole series of loose sts on the R.H. needle. Slip all sts to other end of needle.

Next Row: Sl the 2 sts already worked onto needle and start the cross st thus: *insert the needle into 5th long st, being careful not to twist the st. Knit the 5th loop, draw over the 4 long sts. Knit the 6th, 7th and 8th sts in the same manner, then knit the 4 sts that have been crossed. Repeat from * to last 2 sts, k2.

Repeat last 4 rows, 10 times.

Knit 2 rows.

Cast off.

Lace edging

Cast on 26 sts.

Knit one row.

Row 1: Sl 1, k3, (m3, k1) 16 times, k1, (m2, k2 tog) twice, k1.

Row 2: K3, (p1, k2) twice. *Insert needle into next st purlwise. Slip the st unworked onto R.H. needle, at the same time drop the twisted thread from L.H. needle and absorb it by drawing it into the stitch just slipped, letting the thread into a long loose st*. Repeat *—* until all twisted sts are used and you have the whole series of loose sts on R.H. needle. Slip the last 3 sts onto needle. Slip all sts to other end of needle. Begin by slipping the 9 sts already worked onto R.H. needle. Continue along row thus: *insert needle into 5th long st and knit, slipping it over the 4 sts on the needle*. Repeat *—* to last 3 sts, k3.

Row 3: Sl 1, k27.

Row 4: Cast off 2 sts, k25.

Repeat rows 1–4 until length desired

Cast off

To make up

Lightly press the edging. Join ends neatly. Attach edging to centre, easing the lace at the corners. Make 4 ribbon bows, place at each corner. Insert lavender into completed sachet, using contrasting lining if preferred.

19

Ring Cushion

A beautiful ring cushion designed and knitted by Ruth Rintoule. The intricate lace edging dates from the mid nineteenth century. Overall the cushion is about 36 cm (14 inches) square, with the centre being about 18 cm (7 inches) across and the edging 9 cm (3½ inches) deep.

Materials

1 × 50 g ball DMC 20 cotton

Four pairs of needles:

2.75 mm (12)

2.25 mm (13)

1.75 mm (15)

1.25 mm (18)

Decorative button (Ruth used a pair of doves)

Small pearls

Fine sewing needle and thread

Fibre filling

Lavender

Centre

Using 2.25 mm (13) needles:

Cast on 72 sts. Knit 2 rows.

Row 1: P2, (m1, p4 tog) to last 2 sts, p2.

Row 2: K2, [k1, (k1, p1, k1) into each m1 of previous row] to last 2 sts, k2.

Row 3: Knit.

Repeat rows 1–3 until work measures 18 cm (7 inches) square.

Knit 1 row.

Cast off.

Edging

Using 2.75mm (12) needles:

Cast on 23 sts. Knit 1 row.

Row 1: Sl 1, k2, m1, k2 tog, k1, ★m2, k2 tog. Repeat from ★ 7 times, k1.

Row 2: K1, ★k2, purl 2nd st of m2 of the previous row. Repeat from ★ 7 times, k6.

Row 3: Sl 1, k2, m1, k2 tog, k1, ★m2, k2 tog. Repeat from ★ 11 times, k1.

Row 4: As row 2, repeating from ★ 11 times.

Row 5: Sl 1, k2, m1, k2 tog, k1, ★m2, k2 tog. Repeat from ★ 17 times, k1.

Row 6: As row 2, repeating from ★ 17 times.

Row 7: Sl 1, k2, m1, k2 tog, k56.

Row 8: Cast off 11 sts, k5 (6 sts on needle). Cast off 8 sts, k3 (4 sts on needle). Cast off 7 sts, k3 (4 sts on needle). Cast off 6 sts, k3 (4 sts on needle). Cast off 6 sts, k4 (5 sts on needle).

Repeat rows 1–8 until length required to edge centre square, allowing fullness at corners.

Cast off.

Press the edging. Join ends.

Lace edging for hearts

Using 1.75 mm (15) needles:

Cast on 5 sts (make 2).

Row 1: Sl 1, k1, m1, k2 tog, k1.

Row 2: As row 1.

Row 3: As row 1, working in front, back and front of last st.

Row 4: Sl 1, k1, psso, k1, pass 1st st over k1, m1, k2 tog, k1.

Repeat rows 1–4 twenty-six times.

Cast off.

Handle for back of cushion

Using 1.75 mm (15) needles:

Cast on 10 sts.

Row 1: Sl 1, knit to end of row.

Repeat row 1 until work measures 17 cm (6½ inches).

Cast off.

To make up

Stitch together knitted centre square and fabric square for cushion, leaving an opening for the filling. Stitch

Three Heart Sachets *(instructions on page 62)*

Rosebuds and Pearls, Pompadour and Paulette
(instructions on page 64)

Half-Doll Quartet *(instructions on page 67)*

Antoinette *(instructions on page 70)*

Leaves and Squares Cushion *(instructions on page 72)*

Three Floral Sachets *(instructions on page 74)*

Josephine, Harriet and Hilary *(instructions on page 76)*

Corps de ballet 'Butterflies' *(instructions on page 82)*

60

lace edging to centre square, easing the lace at the corners. Fill the inner cushion with fibre filling and lavender. Close the opening with small stitches. Stitch handle to the edges at the back of the ring cushion and 4 cm (1½ inches) in from each end, leaving sufficient space to put the hand through.

Hearts

(make 2)

Small piece of fine fabric

Small piece of lining if top fabric is sheer

Cut template for heart motif from pattern. Cut fabric for motifs, allowing small turning all round. Turn under seam allowance and stitch. Ease lace around heart shapes and stitch pearls into position.

Stitch finished hearts into position on cushion. Sew decorative button in position to hold the cord (or ribbon if you prefer) which will hold the rings.

Cord

Using 1.75 mm (15) needles:

Cast on 4 sts.

Row 1: Knit.

Slip sts to beginning of row and knit again.

Repeat until length required to tie rings to cushion.

Cast off.

Heart motif template

20

Three Heart Sachets

Three delicate heart-shaped sachets, each lace-trimmed with a different edging, knitted by the author. They were embroidered by Joan Jackson. Joan's embroidery designs are all worked in a spontaneous fashion, relying simply on the use of colour and her skill with the needle. This gives a freedom to her designs lacking in those worked from charts and transfers.

Materials

• SACHET

1 × 50 g ball Anny Blatt cotton (approx. 6-ply)

Pair needles 3 mm (11)

• LACE EDGINGS

1 × 20 g ball DMC Cébélia 10 cotton

Pair needles 2 mm (14)

White silk ribbon 7 mm (¼ inch) wide for sachet hanger

Embroidery and sewing needles

• EMBROIDERY THREADS

– Pansies

Minnamurra stranded, shade 10

DMC stranded cotton 502

Silk ribbon 7 mm (¼ inch) wide

– Cup flowers

DMC 3364

Minnamurra 60 (14) centres

Mill Hill beads 42011 petite

DMC stranded cottons 552, 553, 554, 224, 3608

– Rosebuds

DMC stranded cottons 3364, 224, 223

Silk ribbon 4 mm (1/8 inch) wide

BASIC HEART SACHET

Cast on 2 sts.

Row 1: Knit.

Working in st st, inc both ends of every row until there are 22 sts on needle.

Row 12: Purl.

Row 13: Knit, inc both ends of row.

Row 14: Purl.

Row 15: Knit, inc both ends of row.

Continue in st st for 12 rows.

Row 28: Dec in next st, p9, p2 tog, sl 1, p1, psso, p9, dec in last st.

Row 29: Dec in next st, k9. Turn. Continue on these 10 sts.

Row 30: Dec in next st, p6, dec in last st.

Row 31: Dec in next st, k4, dec in last st.

Row 32: Cast off.

Join yarn to remaining sts. Work other side to correspond.

PANSIES EDGING

Cast on 4 sts.

Row 1: K1, p3.

Row 2: K1, m1, k1 tbl, m1, sl 1, k1, psso.

Row 3: K1, p2, (k1, p1, k1, p1) in next st, p1.

Row 4: Cast off 4 sts, k1, m1, sl 1, k1, psso.

Repeat rows 1–4 until length desired.

Cast off.

CUP FLOWER EDGING

Cast on 4 sts.

Row 1: K1, m1, k2 tog, m2, k1.

Row 2: K2, p1, k1, m1, k2 tog.

Row 3: K1, m1, k2 tog, k3.

Row 4: Cast off 2 sts, k1, m1, k2 tog.

Repeat rows 1–4 until length desired.

Cast off.

ROSEBUDS EDGING

Cast on 4 sts.

Row 1: Sl 1, k1, m2, k2.

Row 2: K3, p1, k2.

Row 3: Sl 1, k5.

Row 4: K6.

Row 5: Sl 1, k1, m2, k2 tog, m2, k2.

Row 6: K3, (p1, k2) twice.

Row 7: Sl 1, k8.

Row 8: Cast off 5 sts, k3.

Repeat rows 1–8 until length desired.

Cast off.

To make up

Stitch sachet together leaving a 5 cm (2 inch) opening. Embroider the sachet with your chosen design. For a personal touch use an embroidered initial, or a monogram, perhaps incorporated into the flower design. Fill with fibre filling and lavender. Stitch the opening together, and add lace edging of your choice, taking care to allow fullness around curves. Attach ribbons to hang sachet if desired.

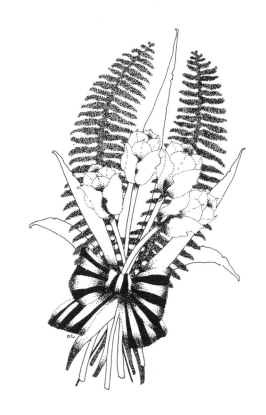

21

Rosebuds and Pearls, Pompadour and Paulette

A dainty square lace-edged sachet delicately embroidered with Rosebuds and Pearls in bullion and lazy daisy stitches, and the half-doll sachets Pompadour (back) and Paulette (front), all designed and knitted by Ruth Rintoule from nineteenth century patterns.

ROSEBUDS AND PEARLS

Materials

1 × 50 g ball DMC Cébélia 40 cotton

Pair needles 1.75 mm (15)

Cotton waffle fabric, 2 pieces approx. 20 cm (8 inches) square

72 small pearls

DMC stranded cottons 776, 503

Needle and thread

Lavender or potpourri

Small amount of soft fibre filling

Press stud

Ribbon for bows

Measurements

Edging 4 cm (1½ inches) wide

Sachet 17 cm (6½ inches) square

Cast on 22 sts.

Row 1: Sl 1, k1, (m1, k2 tog) 3 times, k4, k2 tog, m1, k2, k2 tog, m1, k1, m1, k3 tog.

Row 2: Sl 1, m1, k3, m1, k2 tog, k2, m1, k2 tog, k11.

Row 3: Sl 1, k9, k2 tog, m1, k2, k2 tog, m1, k5, m1, k1.

Row 4: Sl 1, m1, k7, m1, k2 tog, k2, m1, k2 tog, k9.

Row 5: Sl 1, k1, (m1, k2 tog) 3 times, k2 tog, m1, k2, k2 tog, m1, k9, m1, k1.

Row 6: K2 tog, m1, k2 tog, k5, k2 tog, m1, k2, k2 tog, m1, k10.

Row 7: Sl 1, k10, m1, k2 tog, k2, m1, k2 tog, k3, k2 tog, m1, k2 tog.

Row 8: K2 tog, m1, k2 tog, k1, k2 tog, m1, k2, k2 tog, m1, k12.

Row 9: Sl 1, k1, (m1, k2 tog) 3 times, k5, m1, k2 tog, k2, m1, k3 tog, m1, k2 tog.

Row 10: K2 tog, m1, k1, m1, k2, k2 tog, m1, k14.

Row 11: Sl 1, k11, k2 tog, m1, k2, k2 tog, m1, k1, m1, k3 tog.

Repeat rows 2–11 until length desired.

Cast off.

Press the lace. Join ends.

To make up

Work rosebuds within a 10 cm (4½ inch) square in centre of one piece of waffle fabric at even distances, allowing space for pearls in between. Make fabric into sachet 17 cm (6½ inches) square, following basic instructions on page 13, leaving opening to insert lavender sachet.

Gather lace, stitch around sachet, easing at corners. Using organza fabric, stitch an insert to hold lavender or potpourri with a small amount of soft fibre. Place in sachet. Sew on press stud. Attach ribbon bows at sachet corners.

POMPADOUR

Materials

1 × 50 g ball DMC Cébélia 40 cotton

Pair needles 1.25 mm (18)

Small pearls

17 cm (6¾ inch) half doll and base

Fine cotton for sachet

Lavender or potpourri

Soft fibre filling

Needle and thread

Cast on 178 sts. Knit 2 rows.

Row 1: K1, (k2 tog) twice, *(m1, k1) 3 times, m1, (k2 tog) 4 times. Repeat from * to last 8 sts, (m1, k1) 3 times, m1, (k2 tog) twice, k1.

Row 2: Purl.

Rows 3 and 4: Knit.

Repeat rows 1–4 five times.

Row 1: Purl.

Row 2: Knit.

Row 3: Purl.

Row 4: Knit.

Row 5: Purl.

Row 6: Purl.

Repeat rows 1–4 of lace pattern 14 times, then work rows 1 and 2 once.

Shape waist thus:

Row 1: K1, (k2 tog, k2) to end of row.

Knit 3 rows.

Row 5: K1, (k2 tog, k1) to end of row.

Knit 3 rows.

Row 9: K1, (k2 tog) to end of row.

Knit 3 rows.

Row 13: K1, (k2 tog, k1) to last 2 sts, k2 tog.

Knit 8 rows.

Cast off.

Lightly press skirt. Join back seam.

Flowers

Cast on 5 sts.

Row 1: K2, m1, k1, m1, k2.

Row 2: Knit.

Row 3: K3, m1, k2 tog, m1, k2.

Row 4: Knit.

Row 5: K4, m1, k2 tog, m1, k2.

Row 6: Cast off 4 sts. Knit to end of row.

Repeat rows 1–6 five times.

Cast off.

Join ends. Gather to form flower. Stitch pearls in centre if desired.

Place flowers at top of skirt and stitch into position.

Bow

Cast on 3 sts.

Row 1: Knit.

Row 2: Knit, inc each end (5 sts).

Repeat row 1 until length desired. Cast off.

Tie into bow and attach to back of skirt at waistline. (You could use ribbon if you prefer.)

PAULETTE

Materials

1 × 50 g ball DMC 40 cotton

Pair needles 1.25 mm (18)

1.5 metres (1¾ yd) narrow ribbon

Small quantity tiny pearls (optional)

13 cm (5 inch) half doll and base

Sewing needle and thread

Lavender and fibre filling

Fine white fabric for lavender bag

Cast on 50 sts.

Row 1: Sl 1, k2, m1, k2 tog, (k2 tog, m2, sl 1, k1, psso, k2, m1, k2 tog) 5 times, k1, m2, k4.

Row 2: K5, (p1, k3, m1, k2 tog, k2) 5 times, p1, k3, m1, k2 tog, k1.

Row 3: Sl 1, k2, (m1, k2 tog, k6) 5 times, m1, k2 tog, k7.

Row 4: Cast off 2 sts, (k6, m1, k2 tog) 6 times, k1.

Repeat rows 1–4 until work measures approximately 27 cm (10½ inches), or length desired.

Cast off.

Pick up 63 sts along top edge for waistband.

Knit 2 rows.

Next Row: (K1, k2 tog) to end of row.

Knit 14 rows.

Cast off.

To make up

Fold waistband over and stitch. Join skirt seam. Thread lengths of ribbon through holes in skirt and waistband. Tie a bow at waist. Stitch pearls down skirt seam for an added touch (optional).

22

Half-Doll Quartet

(Pictured on page 58.) At the front is Beatrice, a Dutch-style half doll, with Thomasina, an interesting Japanese half doll. Camilla in the centre is wearing an intricate Vandyke overskirt with a detachable fluted frill underneath, with the tiny Mignon at the back. Sachets designed and knitted by the author. Beatrice, Thomasina and Mignon from the Pat Walsh collection, Camilla from the author's collection.

BEATRICE

Materials

Knitted base approx. 12 cm (4½ inches) high, made following instructions on page 13

1 × 20 g ball DMC 20 cotton

Pair needles 2 mm (14)

9 cm (3½ inch) half doll

Lavender and filling for base

Sewing cotton and needle

Fine silk ribbons for waist

Cast on 30 sts.

Row 1: K28, m1, k2 tog.

Row 2: K1, p14. Turn.

Row 3: K1, (m1, k2 tog) 7 times.

Row 4: K1, p14, k10. Turn.

Row 5: K23, m1, k2 tog.

Row 6: K30.

Row 7: K15, p13, m1, k2 tog.

Row 8: K15. Turn.

Row 9: P13, m1, k2 tog.

Row 10: K25. Turn.

Row 11: K23, m1, k2 tog.

Row 12: K1, p14, k15.

Row 13: K16, (m1, k2 tog) 7 times.

Row 14: K1, p14. Turn.

Row 15: K13, m1, k2 tog.

Row 16: K25. Turn.

Row 17: K10, p13, m1, k2 tog.

Row 18: K30.

Row 19: K15, p13, m1, k2 tog.

Row 20: K30.

Repeat rows 1–20 until length desired.

Cast off.

To make up

Put knitted sachet base and half doll together. Press Beatrice lace, avoiding fluted section, and fit over base. Thread piece of yarn along top of skirt and draw up, adjusting to fit doll's waist. Add ribbon, tie in bow at the back.

THOMASINA

Materials

Knitted base 18 cm (7 inches) high, made following instructions on page 13

1 × 20 g ball DMC 20 cotton

Pair needles 2 mm (14)

7 cm (3 inch) half doll

Lavender and filling for base

Sewing thread and needle

Small ribbon bow

Cast on 29 sts.

Row 1: Knit.

Row 2: K5, p16, (m1, k2 tog) 3 times, m1, k2.

Row 3: K25. Turn.

Row 4: P17, (m1, k2 tog) 3 times, m1, k2.

Row 5: K26. Turn.

Row 6: K18, (m1, k2 tog) 3 times, m1, k2.

Row 7: K9, p18. Turn.

Row 8: K1, (m1, k2 tog) 12 times, m1, k2.

Row 9: K9, p19, k5.

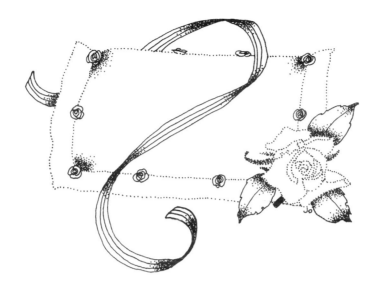

Row 10: Knit.

Row 11: Cast off 4 sts, knit to end of row.

Repeat rows 2–11 twenty-two times.

Cast off.

Note that this lace is reversible.

To make up

Put knitted sachet base and half doll together.

Press Thomasina lace, avoiding fluted section, and fit over base. Thread piece of yarn along top of skirt and draw up, adjusting to fit doll's waist.

Place small bow on hip.

CAMILLA

Materials

Knitted base 10 cm (4 inches) high, made following instructions on page 13

1 × 50 g ball DMC 20 cotton

Pair needles 1.50 mm (16)

5 cm (2 inch) half doll

Length of narrow white ribbon

Sewing needle and cotton

Lavender and filling

Special abbreviation
mh = make hole, worked thus: sl 1, k1, psso, (k1, pass previous st over) twice

Overskirt

Cast on 30 sts. Knit one row.

Row 1: K3, (mh, k2) 3 times, mh, k5.

Row 2: Sl 1, k5, (m3, k3) 4 times.

Row 3: K4, (p1, k5) 3 times, p1, k7.

Row 4: Sl 1, k29. Cast on 3 sts.

Row 5: K3, (mh, k2) 3 times, mh, k8.

Row 6: Sl 1, k8, (m3, k3) 4 times.

Row 7: K4, (p1, k5) 3 times, p1, k10.

Row 8: Sl 1, k32. Cast on 3 sts.

Row 9: K3, (mh, k2) 3 times, mh, k11.

Row 10: Sl 1, k11, (m3, k3) 4 times.

Row 11: K4, (p1, k5) 3 times, p1, k13.

Row 12: Sl 1, k35. Cast on 3 sts.

Row 13: K3, (mh, k2) 3 times, mh, k14.

Row 14: Sl 1, k3, sl 1, k1, psso, m2, k2 tog, k7, (m3, k3) 4 times.

Row 15: K4, (p1, k5) 3 times, p1, k10, p1, k5.

Row 16: Sl 1, k1, (sl 1, k1, psso, m2, k2 tog) twice, k29. Cast on 3 sts.

Row 17: K3, (mh, k2) 3 times, mh, k9, (p1, k3) twice.

Row 18: Sl 1, k3, sl 1, k1, psso, m2, k2 tog, k10, (m3, k3) 4 times.

Row 19: K4, (p1, k5) 3 times, p1, k13, p1, k5.

Row 20: Sl 1, k1, (sl 1, k1, psso, m2, k2 tog) twice, k32.

Row 21: Cast off 3 sts, k2, (mh, k2) 3 times, mh, k6, (p1, k3) twice.

Row 22: Sl 1, k3, sl 1, k1, psso, m2, k2 tog, k7, (m3, k3) 4 times.

Row 23: K4, (p1, k5) 3 times, p1, k10, p1, k5.

Row 24: Sl 1, k38.

Row 25: Cast off 3 sts, k2, (mh, k2) 3 times, mh, k11.

Row 26: Sl 1, k11, (m3, k3) 4 times.

Row 27: K4, (p1, k5) 3 times, p1, k13.

Row 28: Sl 1, k35.

Row 29: Cast off 3 sts, k2, (mh, k2) 3 times, mh, k8.

Row 30: Sl 1, k8, (m3, k3) 4 times.

Row 31: K4, (p1, k5) 3 times, p1, k10.

Row 32: Sl 1, k32.

Row 33: Cast off 3 sts, k2, (mh, k2) 3 times, mh, k5.

Row 34: Sl 1, k5, (m3, k3) 4 times.

Row 35: K4, (p1, k5) 3 times, p1, k7.

Row 36: Sl 1, k29. Cast on 3 sts.

Row 37: K3, (mh, k2) 3 times, mh, k8.

Row 38: Sl 1, k8, (m3, k3) 4 times.

Row 39: K4, (p1, k5) 3 times, p1, k10.

Row 40: Sl 1, k32. Cast on 3 sts.

Row 41: K3, (mh, k2) 3 times, mh, k11.

Row 42: Sl 1, k11, (m3, k3) 4 times.

Row 43: K4, (p1, k5) 3 times, p1, k13.

Row 44: Sl 1, k35. Cast on 3 sts.

Repeat rows 13–44 for a straight piece of lace of the length desired.

Cast off.

Lightly press.

Pick up approx 88 sts along straight edge of lace.

Knit 2 rows.

Next Row: (K1, k2 tog) to end of row.

Knit 2 rows.

Next Row: (K1, k2 tog) to end of row.

Make row of ribbon holes thus:

K1, m1, k2 tog to end of row.

Knit 3 rows.

Cast off.

Detachable fluted frill

Cast on 18 sts.

Row 1: Knit.

Row 2: P14. Turn (4 sts left on needle).

Row 3: Sl 1, k9, k2 tog, m2, k2.

Row 4: P14, (dropping 2nd loop of the m2 of the previous row). Turn.

Row 5: Sl 1, k13.

Row 6: Knit.

Row 7: K4, p14.

Row 8: K1, k2 tog, m2, k11. Turn.

Row 9: Sl 1, p13, (dropping 2nd loop as before).

Row 10: K18.

Repeat rows 1–10 until length required to balance the Vandyke edge of the overskirt.

Cast off.

To make up

Thread narrow ribbon through holes at top of overskirt and the fluted frill, if you choose to make it. Draw up the ribbon of the overskirt and adjust to doll's waist, tying in a bow at the back. Draw up the ribbon in the fluted frill and tie or stitch into place around lavender base. The fluted frill complements the Vandyke hemline of the Camilla lace overskirt.

MIGNON

Materials

1 × 20 g ball DMC 20 cotton

Pair needles 2 mm (14)

4 cm (1¾ inch) half doll

Knitted base 6 cm (2½ inches) high, made following pattern

Cast on 41 sts.

Row 1: K1, (m1, sl 1, k2 tog, psso, m1, k1) to end of row.

Row 2: Knit.

Repeat rows 1 and 2 ten times.

Cast off thus:

Row 1: P1, (p2 tog) to end of row.

Row 2: K1, (k2 tog) to end of row.

Cut yarn, leaving sufficient to thread through stitches on needle, gather up and tighten off.

To make up

Thread ribbons through holes at waist if desired. Sew side seams. Stuff the sachet with small amounts of fibre filling and lavender. Thread yarn through cast-on stitches, draw up to form cylindrical base. Insert tiny porcelain doll at top. Fasten securely. Tie cluster of ribbons around waist.

23

Antoinette

Ruth Rintoule designed and knitted this elegant skirt for the Antoinette half doll sachet.

Materials

1 half doll

1 × 50 g ball DMC 20 cotton

Pair needles 1.75 mm (15)

1 m (40 inches) narrow blue ribbon

50 cm (20 inches) narrow white ribbon

Fine white fabric for underskirt sachet (see page 14)

Press stud

Sewing needle and cotton

Skirt

Cast on 31 sts. Knit one row.

Row 1: Sl 1, k6, m1, k2 tog, k3, k2 tog, m2, k2 tog, k3, (m1, k2 tog) 4 times, k1, m1, k2 tog, k1.

Row 2: M2, p1, k16, p1, k13.

Row 3: Sl 1, k5, (m1, k2 tog) twice, k10, (m1, k2 tog) 3 times, k2 tog, m1, k1, m1, k2 tog, k1.

Row 4: M2, p1, k31.

Row 5: Sl 1, k4, (m1, k2 tog) 3 times, k3, k2 tog, m2, k2 tog, k3, (m1, k2 tog) twice, k2 tog, m1, k3, m1, k2 tog, k1.

Row 6: M2, p1, k16, p1, k15.

Row 7: Sl 1, k3, (m1, k2 tog) 4 times, k10, m1, (k2 tog) twice, m1, k5, m1, k2 tog, k1.

Row 8: M2, p1, k33.

Row 9: Sl 1, k4, (m1, k2 tog) 4 times, k3, k2 tog, m2, k2 tog, k3, k2 tog, m1, k7, m1, k2 tog, k1.

Row 10: M2, p1, k16, p1, k17.

Row 11: Sl 1, k5, (m1, k2 tog) 4 times, k8, k2 tog, m1, k9, m1, k2 tog, k1.

Row 12: M2, p1, k35

Row 13: S1 1, k6, (m1, k2 tog) 4 times, k6, k2 tog, m1, k11, m1, k2 tog, k1.

Row 14: M2, p1, k36.

Row 15: Sl 1, k7, (m1, k2 tog) 4 times, k4, k2 tog, m1, k5, k2 tog, m2, k6, m1, k2 tog, k2.

Row 16: M2, p1, k9, p1, k28.

Row 17: Sl 1, k8, (m1, k2 tog) 4 times, k2, k2 tog, m1, k4, (k2 tog, m2, k2 tog) twice, k4, m1, k2 tog, k1.

Row 18: M2, p1, k8, p1, k3, p1, k26.

Row 19: Sl 1, k2, k2 tog, m2, k2 tog, k3, (m1, k2 tog) 4 times, k2 tog, m1, k7, k2 tog, m2, k2 tog, k7, m1, k2 tog, k1.

Row 20: M1, k2 tog, k10, p1, k23, p1, k4.

Row 21: Sl 1, k10, (m1, k2 tog) 4 times, k1, m1, k2 tog, k3, (k2 tog, m2, k2 tog) twice, k3, k2 tog, m1, k2 tog, k1.

Row 22: M1, k2 tog, k7, p1, k3, p1, k26.

Row 23: Sl 1, k4, k2 tog, m2, k2 tog, k3, (m1, k2 tog) 4 times, k1, m1, k2 tog, k4, k2 tog, m2, k2 tog, k4, k2 tog, m1, k2 tog, k1.

Row 24: M1, k2 tog, k8, p1, k21, p1, k6.

Row 25: Sl 1, k12, (m1, k2 tog) 4 times, k1, m1, k2 tog, k10, k2 tog, m1, k2 tog, k1.

Row 26: M1, k2 tog, k36.

Row 27: Sl 1, k6, k2 tog, m2, k2 tog, k3, (m1, k2 tog) 4 times, k1, m1, k2 tog, k8, k2 tog, m1, k2 tog, k1.

Row 28: M1, k2 tog, k26, p1, k8.

Row 29: Sl 1, k14, (m1, k2 tog) 4 times, k1, m1, k2 tog, k6, k2 tog, m1, k2 tog, k1.

Row 30: M1, k2 tog, k34.

Row 31: Sl 1, k8, k2 tog, m2, k2 tog, k3, (m1, k2 tog) 4 times, k1, m1, k2 tog, k4, k2 tog, m1, k2 tog, k1.

Row 32: M1, k2 tog, k22, p1, k10.

Row 33: Sl 1, k16, (m1, k2 tog) 4 times, k1, m1, k2 tog, k2, k2 tog, m1, k2 tog, k1.

Row 34: M1, k2 tog, k32.

Row 35: Sl 1, k10, k2 tog, m2, k2 tog, k3, (m1, k2 tog) 4 times, k1, m1, (k2 tog) twice. Pass 1st k2 tog over, m1, k2 tog, k1.

Row 36: M1, k2 tog, k17, p1, k12.

Row 37: Sl 1, k14, k2 tog, k2, (m1, k2 tog) 4 times, k1, m1, k2 tog, k2.

Row 38: M1, k2 tog, k29.

Repeat rows 1–38 seven times. Cast off.

Pick up and knit 77 sts along the top edge of lace.

Knit 2 rows.

Row 3: K1, *m1, k3 tog*. Repeat from * to last st, k1.

Row 4: Knit (52 sts).

Row 5: K1, *m1, k3 tog*. Repeat from * to end.

Row 6: Knit (35 sts).

Row 7: K1, *m1, k2 tog*. Repeat from * to end.

Row 8: Knit.

Repeat rows 7 and 8.

Row 11: Knit.

Cast off.

Underskirt

Make a basic underskirt sachet following the instructions on page 14.

To make up

Join the Antoinette lace together, drawing in the top to fit the doll's waist. Fit the lavender insert inside the underskirt. Sew press stud to underskirt to close the opening. Cut the narrow blue ribbon into equal lengths and plait with the white ribbon to trim the doll's waist; tie in bows at the back.

24

Leaves and Squares Cushion

An attractive design in a thicker thread from a bedspread motif of the nineteenth century. The use of fine needles makes a firmer fabric than usual, enhancing the raised leaf motif of the reversible cushion. This attractive cushion sachet, approximately 25 cm (10 inches) square, was knitted by Ruth Tyrie.

Materials

4 × 50 g balls DMC Hermina cotton

Pair needles 2 mm (14)

Length of white ribbon

White fabric for cushion insert

Fibre filling

Lavender

Sewing needle and thread

Cast on 3 sts.

Row 1: M1, k3.

Row 2: M1, k4.

Row 3: M1, k2, m1, k1, m1, k2.

Row 4: M1, k2, p3, k3.

Row 5: M1, k4, m1, k1, m1, k4.

Row 6: M1, k3, p5, k4.

Row 7: M1, k6, m1, k1, m1, k6.

Row 8: M1, k4, p7, k5.

Row 9: M1, k8, m1, k1, m1, k8.

Row 10: M1, k5, p9, k6.

Row 11: M1, k10, m1, k1, m1, k10.

Row 12: M1, k6, p11, k7.

Row 13: M1, k12, m1, k1, m1, k12.

Row 14: M1, k7, p13, k8.

Row 15: M1, k8, sl 1, k1, psso, k9, k2 tog, k8.

Row 16: M1, k8, p11, k9.

Row 17: M1, k9, sl 1, k1, psso, k7, k2 tog, k9.

Row 18: M1, k9, p9, k10.

Row 19: M1, k10, sl 1, k1, psso, k5, k2 tog, k10.

Row 20: M1, k10, p7, k11.

Row 21: M1, k11, sl 1, k1, psso, k3, k2 tog, k11.

Row 22: M1, k11, p5, k12.

Row 23: M1, k12, sl 1, k1, psso, k1, k2 tog, k12.

Row 24: M1, k12, p3, k13.

Row 25: M1, k13, sl 2, k1, p2sso, k13.

Row 26: M1, k1, purl to end.

Rows 27, 28 and 29: M1, knit to end.

Repeat rows 26 to 29 five times and row 26 once (53 sts).

Row 51: M1, (k2 tog, m1). Repeat to last st, k1.

Row 52: As row 26.

Row 53: M1, k1, (m1, k2 tog). Repeat to last 2 sts, k2.

Row 54: As row 26.

Row 55: As row 53.

Row 56: As row 26.

Rows 57, 58 and 59: As row 27.

Row 60: As row 26.

Rows 61 and 62: As row 27.

Row 63: M1, k1, p1, (m1, k1, m1, p9). Repeat to last 3 sts, m1, k1, m1, p1, k1.

Row 64: M1, k2, (p3, k9). Repeat to last 6 sts, p3, k3.

Row 65: M1, k1, p2, (k1, m1, k1, m1, k1, p9). Repeat to last 6 sts, k1, m1, k1, m1, k1, p2, k1.

Row 66: M1, k3, (p5, k9). Repeat to last 9 sts, p5, k4.

Row 67: M1, k1, p3, (k2, m1, k1, m1, k2, p9). Repeat to last 4 sts, p3, k1.

Row 68: M1, k4, (p7, k9). Repeat to last 12 sts, p7, k5.

Row 69: M1, k1, p4, (k3, m1, k1, m1, k3, p9). Repeat to last 5 sts, p4, k1.

Row 70: M1, k5, (p9, k9). Repeat to last 15 sts, p9, k6.

Row 71: M1, k1, p5, (sl 1, k1, psso, k5, k2 tog, p9). Repeat to last 6 sts, p5, k1.

Row 72: M1, k6, (p7, k9). Repeat to last 14 sts, p7, k7.

Row 73: M1, k1, p6, (sl 1, k1, psso, k3, k2 tog, p9). Repeat to last 7 sts, p6, k1.

Row 74: M1, k7, (p5, k9). Repeat to last 13 sts, p5, k8.

Row 75: M1, k1, p7, (sl 1, k1, psso, k1, k2 tog, p9). Repeat to last 8 sts, p7, k1.

Row 76: M1, k8, (p3, k9). Repeat to end of row.

Row 77: M1, k1, p8, (sl 2, k1, p2sso, p9). Repeat to last 9 sts, p8, k1.

Row 78: As row 26.

Row 79: As row 27.

Row 80: As row 26.

Row 81: As row 27.

Cast off.

Repeat rows 1–81 seven times to make the eight triangles needed for the cushion.

To make up

Lightly press each piece, avoiding the raised design. Join four triangles to make a square by oversewing through the corresponding loops formed by the made stitches. Join the other four triangles for the back of the cushion. Sew front and back squares together, leaving an opening large enough to insert an inner sachet filled with fibre filling and a lavender insert. Neatly close opening. Finish with small ribbon bows at each corner if desired.

25

Three Floral Sachets

(Pictured on page 60.) Violet is embroidered in DMC silk ribbons on a basic linen sachet by Joan Jackson. The sachet is 13 cm (5 inches) square, and is edged with lace knitted by the author. Heartsease is a basic square sachet 14 cm (5½ inches) across with a classic lace edging 5 cm (2 inches) wide, embroidered by Joan Jackson and edged with lace knitted by the author. The sachet centre is edged with lace braid. Roseleaf is made in silk dupion, embroidered by Joan Jackson in delicate colours enhanced by the lace knitted by the author. This sachet is 18 cm (7 inches) square.

VIOLET

Materials

1 × 20 g ball DMC 80 cotton

Pair needles 1.25 mm (18)

Sewing thread and fine needle for attaching lace

DMC silk ribbons for embroidery, and for threading through lace

50 cm fine linen for sachet

Lavender

Fibre filling

Cast on 31 sts.

Row 1: Sl 1, k1, k2 tog, m2, k2 tog, k1, (m1, k2 tog) twice, k2 tog, m2, k2 tog, k1, m2, k2 tog, (m1, k2 tog) 6 times, k1.

Row 2: K15, p1, k3, p1, k8, p1, k3.

Row 3: Sl 1, k6, (m1, k2 tog) twice, k5, m2, k2 tog, (m1, k2 tog) 6 times, m1, k2.

Row 4: Cast off 3 sts, k13, p1, k16.

Repeat rows 1–4 until length desired.

Cut linen into two pieces, with seam allowances, to make a sachet 13 cm (5 inches) square. Embroider the front and make up sachet, leaving an opening for the filling. Press the lace, and attach to the embroidered sachet, allowing ample fullness around the corners. Thread ribbon through holes in lace and stitch ends together. Alternatively, use four lengths and tie a bow at each corner.

HEARTSEASE

Materials

2 × 20 g balls DMC Cordonnet Special 100 cotton

Pair needles 1.25 mm (18)

Fine sewing thread and needle for attaching lace to sachet

Lace braid of length required (see pattern)

DMC stranded cottons:

90, 115, 316, 340, 462, 550, 552, 727, 937, 950, 3345, 3346, 3363, 3747

Perle No.5 black 340, No.8 102

Rayon threads 225, 209

Medici 2-ply wool, dyed in variegated shades of purple

Silk ribbon for bow (optional)

Cast on 26 sts.

Row 1: K2 tog, k1, m1, k2 tog, k5, k2 tog, m1, k2 tog, k9, m1, k2 tog, k1.

Row 2: Sl 1, k2, m1, k2 tog, k1, (k2 tog, m1) twice, k2 tog, k2, m1, k2 tog, k3, k2 tog, m1, k3.

Row 3: M1, k4, m1, k2 tog, k1, k2 tog, m1, k11, m1, k2 tog, k1.

Row 4: Sl 1, k2, m1, k2 tog, k3, (m1, k2 tog) twice, k3, m1, sl 1, k2 tog, psso, m1, k6.

Row 5: M1, k1, k2 tog, m2, k18, m1, k2 tog, k1.

Row 6: Sl 1, k2, m1, k2 tog, k4, (m1, k2 tog) twice, k9, p1, k3.

Row 7: K1, (k2 tog, m2) twice, k2 tog, k16, m1, k2 tog, k1.

Row 8: Sl 1, k2, m1, k2 tog, k5, (m1, k2 tog) twice, k7, (p1, k2) twice.

Row 9: K2 tog, k1, k2 tog, m2, k2 tog, k3, m1, k1, m1, k2 tog, k11, m1, k2 tog, k1.

Row 10: Sl 1, k2, m1, k2 tog, k3, (k2 tog, m1) twice, (k3, m1) twice k2 tog, k3, p1, k2 tog, k1.

Row 11: K2 tog, k3, k2 tog, m1, k5, m1, k2 tog, k10, m1, k2 tog, k1.

Row 12: Sl 1, k2, m1, k2 tog, k2, (k2 tog, m1) twice, k3, m1, k7, m1, k2 tog, k1, k2 tog.

Repeat rows 1–12 until length required to edge sachet, allowing for extra fullness at corners.

Cast off.

HEARTSEASE LACE BRAID

Materials

1 × 20 g ball DMC Cordonnet Special 10 cotton

Pair needles 1.75 mm (15)

The braid consists of a one-row pattern, worked thus:

Cast on 3 sts.

M1, k2 tog, k1.

Repeat the row until length desired.

Cast off.

To make up

Cut fabric into two pieces, with seam allowances, to make a sachet 14 cm (5½ inches) square. Embroider the front and make up sachet, leaving an opening for the filling. Press the lace, and attach to the embroidered sachet, allowing ample fullness around the corners. Attach a length of Heartsease lace braid around edge of fabric centre (see photograph).

ROSELEAF

Materials

1 ball DMC 12 cotton

Pair needles 1.25 mm (18)

2 pieces silk dupion approx. 20 cm (8 inches) square

DMC embroidery threads 221, 223, 224, 225, 727, 800

Madeira metallic silver thread

Embroidery needle

Lavender

Filling

Fine sewing needle and thread

Cast on 10 sts.

Row 1: Sl 1, k2, m1, k2 tog, (m2, k2 tog) twice, k1.

Row 2: K3, (p1, k2) twice, m1, k2 tog, k1.

Row 3: Sl 1, k2, m1, k2 tog, k2, (m2, k2 tog) twice, k1.

Row 4: K3, p1, k2, p1, k4, m1, k2 tog, k1.

Row 5: Sl 1, k2, m1, k2 tog, k4, (m2, k2 tog) twice, k1.

Row 6: K3, p1, k2, p1, k6, m1, k2 tog, k1.

Row 7: Sl 1, k2, m1, k2 tog, k11.

Row 8: Cast off 6 sts, k6, m1, k2 tog, k1.

Repeat rows 1–8 until length desired.

Cast off.

To make up

Embroider one piece of the silk dupion and make up sachet 18 cm (7 inches) square, leaving an opening for the filling. Press the lace, and attach to the embroidered sachet, allowing ample fullness around the corners.

Trim corners with ribbon bows if desired.

26

Josephine, Harriet and Hilary

(Pictured page 60.) Harriet, in her lace-trimmed fine linen skirt which serves as a pin or brooch holder, is flanked on the left by Hilary, a Japanese half doll with her original base enhanced by a length of knitted lace. On the right is Josephine, a delicate half doll of Continental porcelain, in a ribboned gown. Josephine and Harriet from the author's collection, Hilary from the Patricia Walsh collection.

HARRIET

Materials

Fine white linen 51 × 23 cm (20 × 9 inches)

1 × 20 g ball DMC 10 cotton

Pair needles 2 mm (14)

18 cm (7 inch) half doll with base

Lace braid to trim waist

Narrow silk ribbon for bow

Sewing needle and thread

Lavender and fibre filling for base/insert

Cast on 8 sts.

Row 1: Sl 1, k1, [m1, p2 tog, (k1, p1, k1) in next st] twice.

Row 2: (K3, m1, p2 tog) twice, k2.

Row 3: Sl 1, k1, (m1, p2 tog, k3) twice.

Row 4: (Cast off 2 sts, m1, p2 tog) twice, k2.

Repeat rows 1–4 until length desired.

Lace braid for waist

Cast on 3 sts.

Work the one-row pattern thus:

M1, k2 tog, k1.

Repeat until desired length.

Cast off.

To make up

Fold the piece of linen in half lengthwise. Press right sides together. Sew narrow seam at each end, turn to right side, press again. Stitch gathering thread around top, trim the edges, draw up thread to fit the doll's waist. Press lace. Stitch around the bottom of the skirt with small stitches. Fasten doll into lavender base, adjust linen overskirt and sew the lace braid around waist. The back remains open, fastened with ribbon bows, one at the waist, two more to lace line if desired. Attach green ribbon bow on left hip, allowing ends to trail.

If you wish to use the doll as a pin holder, the double fabric of the skirt gives a firm surface to anchor the pins.

HILARY

Materials

Lavender base and doll 15 cm (6 inches) high, with original base

1 × 20 g ball DMC 20 cotton

Pair needles 2 mm (14)

6 cm (2½ inch) half doll

Lavender

Sewing thread and needle

Fine ribbon for double bow on hip

NB Read this pattern with care.

Cast on 36 sts.

Row 1: M1, k2 tog, k15. Slip the 3rd, 4th, 5th and 6th sts on L.H. needle over the 1st and 2nd sts tog, m2, k2, which are the 2 sts over which the 4 sts were slipped, m2, k3, sl 4 over 2, m2, k2, m2, k4.

Row 2: Sl 1, k4, p4, k5, p4, k4, m2, k2 tog, k12.

Row 3: M1, k2 tog, k12, p1, k22.

Row 4: Sl 1, (k3, p6) twice, k18.

Row 5: M1, k2 tog, k35.

Row 6: Sl 1, (k3, p6) twice, k3, (m2, k2 tog) twice, k11.

Row 7: M1, k2 tog, k11, p1, k2, p1, k22.

Row 8: Sl 1, (k3, p6) twice, k20.

Row 9: M1, k2 tog, k18, slip 4 over 2, m2, k2, m2, k3,

Basket Cushion *(instructions on page 85)*

Morwenna and the Dancers *(instructions on page 87)*

Reseda *(instructions on page 90)*

Red Rose *(instructions on page 91)*

Alexia *(instructions on page 92)*

79

Spanish Point Lace (*instructions on page 93*)

slip 4 over 2, m2, k2, m2, k4.

Row 10: Sl 1, k4, p4, k5, p4, k4, (m2, k2 tog) 3 times, k11.

Row 11: M1, k2 tog, k11, (p1, k2) twice, p1, k22.

Row 12: Sl 1, (k3, p6) twice, k23.

Row 13: M1, k2 tog, k40.

Row 14: Sl 1, (k3, p6) twice, k3, (m2, k2 tog) 4 times, k12.

Row 15: M1, k2 tog, k12, (p1, k2) 3 times, p1, k22.

Row 16: Sl 1, (k3, p6) twice, k25. Slip 9 sts over 2 sts. Knit tog the 2 sts over which the 9 sts were slipped, k2.

Repeat rows 1–16 until length desired.

Cast off.

To make up

If you are using an original base and doll, give her a fresh lavender insert.

Press lace lightly. Thread cotton through top of lace. Draw up and tie around doll's waist. Place silk ribbon bow on hip.

JOSEPHINE

Materials

Knitted base and doll 14 cm (5½ inches) high

1 × 10 g ball DMC 12 cotton, B5200 brilliant white

Pair needles 1.25 mm (18)

4 cm (1½ inch) half doll

2.5 metres (2¾ yd) fine ribbon

Sewing needle and cotton

Lavender and filling

Cast on 26 sts.

Row 1: Sl 1, k2, m1, (k2 tog) twice, m2, sl 1, k1, psso, k3, m1, (k2 tog) twice, m2, sl 1, k1, psso, k4, m1, k2 tog, m1, k2 (27 sts).

Row 2: M1, k2 tog, k9, p1, k8, p1, k6.

Row 3: Sl 1, k20, (m1, k2 tog) twice, m1, k2.

Row 4: M1, k2 tog, k26.

Row 5: Sl 1, k2, m1, (k2 tog) twice, m2, sl 1, k1, psso, k3, m1, (k2 tog) twice, m2, sl 1, k1, psso, k2, (m1, k2 tog) 3 times, m1, k2.

Row 6: M1, k2 tog, k11, p1, k8, p1, k6.

Row 7: Sl 1, k18, (m1, k2 tog) 4 times, m1, k2 (30 sts).

Row 8: M1, k2 tog, k28.

Row 9: Sl 1, k2, m1, (k2 tog) twice, m2, sl 1, k1, psso, k3, m1, (k2 tog) twice, m2, sl 1, k1, psso, (m1, k2 tog) 5 times, m1, k2.

Row 10: M1, k2 tog, k13, p1, k8, p1, k6.

Row 11: Sl 1, k17, k2 tog, (m1, k2 tog) 5 times, k1.

Row 12: M1, k2 tog, k28.

Row 13: Sl 1, k2, m1, (k2 tog) twice, m2, sl 1, k1, psso, k3, m1, (k2 tog) twice, m2, sl 1, k1, psso, k1, k2 tog, (m1, k2 tog) 4 times, k1.

Row 14: M1, k2 tog, k11, p1, k8, p1, k6.

Row 15: Sl 1, k19, k2 tog, (m1, k2 tog) 3 times, k1.

Row 16: M1, k2 tog, k26.

Row 17: Sl 1, k2, m1, (k2 tog) twice, m2, sl 1, k1, psso, k3, m1, (k2 tog) twice, m2, sl 1, k1, psso, k3, k2 tog, (m1, k2 tog) twice, k1.

Row 18: M1, k2 tog, k9, p1, k8, p1, k6.

Row 19: Sl 1, k21, k2 tog, m1, k2 tog, k1.

Row 20: M1, k2 tog, k24.

Repeat rows 1–20 until length desired.

Cast off.

To make up

Fix knitted lavender sachet and half doll together.

Lightly press lace. Thread five lengths of ribbon through holes, leaving ample ribbon to tie into generous bows at back of skirt. Gently draw in ribbon at waist to fit.

27

Corps de ballet 'Butterflies'

(Pictured on page 60.) Clockwise from the front are Cressida, a 1930s style half doll, then Winsome, another delightful 1930s half doll, finely modelled, possible German. Perdita comes next, with no mark to identify the maker. All three dolls are charming in their new roles as lavender sachets. Cressida and Winsome from the Pat Walsh collection, Perdita from the author's collection.

CRESSIDA

Materials

Lavender base 15 cm (6 inches) in diameter, made following instructions on page 13

1 × 50 g DMC 20 cotton

Pair needles 2 mm (14)

10 cm (4 inch) half doll

Net and fine cotton for base

Lavender and filling

Sewing cotton and needle

Ribbon to thread through holes and tie into generous bow at back

Cast on 27 sts.

Row 1: Sl 1, k13, m1, k2, m1, (k2 tog) twice, m1, k2 tog, m1, k2, m2, k2 tog, k1.

Row 2: K3, p1, k2, p20. Turn, leaving 3 sts on needle.

Row 3: K12, m1, k2 tog, k1, k2 tog, m1, k1, m1, k2 tog, m1, k6.

Row 4: K6, p21. Turn, leaving 3 sts on needle.

Row 5: K11, m1, k2 tog, m1, s11, k2 tog, psso, m1, k3, m1, k2 tog, m1, k2, m2, k2 tog, m2, k2.

Row 6: K3, (p1, k2) twice, p22, k3.

Row 7: Sl 1, k2, p12, m1, k2 tog, m1, (k2 tog) twice, m1, k2, m1, k2 tog, m1, k9.

Row 8: Cast off 4 sts, k4 (not counting sts on needle after cast-off), p11, k12. Turn, leaving 3 sts on needle.

Row 9: P11, (m1, k2 tog) 3 times, k1, k2 tog, m1, k1, m1, k2 tog, m1, k2, m2, k2 tog, k1,

Row 10: K3, p1, k2, p13, k11. Turn.

Row 11: P12, (m1, k2 tog) twice, m1, s11, k2 tog, psso, m1, k3, m1, k2 tog, m1, k6,

Row 12: K6, p13, k15.

Row 13: Sl 1, k12, k2 tog, (m1, k2 tog) 3 times, k2 tog, m1, k2, (m1, k2 tog) twice, k1, m2, k2 tog, m2, k2.

Row 14: K3, (p1, k2) twice, p24. Turn.

Row 15: K10, k2 tog, k1, m1, k2 tog, m1, k1, m1, k2 tog, k1, k2 tog, (m1, k2 tog) twice, k8.

Row 16: Cast off 4 sts, k4, p23. Turn.

Row 17: K10, (k2 tog, m1) twice, k3, m1, sl 1, k2 tog, psso, (m1, k2 tog) twice, k1, m2, k2 tog, k1.

Row 18: K3, p1, k2, p22, k3.

Row 19: Sl 1, k2, p9, p2 tog, m1, k2 tog, m1, k2, m1, (k2 tog) twice, (m1, k2 tog) twice, k5.

Row 20: K6, p11, k10. Turn.

Row 21: P10, p2 tog, m1, k1, m1, k2 tog, k1, k2 tog, (m1, k2 tog) twice, k1 m2, k2 tog, m2, k2.

Row 22: K3, p1, k2, p1, k2, p9, k11. Turn.

Row 23: P9, p2 tog, m1, k3, m1, sl 1, k2 tog, psso, (m1, k2 tog) twice, k8.

Row 24: Cast off 4 sts, k4, p9, k13.

Repeat rows 1–24 twenty times.

Cast off.

To make up

Fix lavender sachet and half doll together. Thread ribbon through holes at top of Cressida lace. Tie at back. Adjust lace skirt evenly around lavender sachet.

WINSOME

Materials

Knitted base 10 cm (4 inches) high, made following instructions on page 13

Net for underskirt

4 cm (1¾ inch) half doll

Silk ribbon to tie at waist

Skirt measures approx. 16.5 cm (6½") in diameter

Lavender

Fibre filling

Sewing cotton and needle

Cast on 25 sts.

Row 1: Sl 1, k19, m1, p2 tog, k1, m1, k2.

Row 2: K4, m1, p2 tog, k18. Turn.

Row 3: Sl 1, k17, m1, p2 tog, k2, m1, k2.

Row 4: K5, m1, p2 tog, k16. Turn.

Row 5: Sl 1, k15, m1, p2 tog, k3, m1, k2.

Row 6: K6, m1, p2 tog, k14. Turn.

Row 7: Sl 1, k13, m1, p2 tog, k2 tog, m2, k2, m1, k2.

Row 8: K6, p1, k1, m1, p2 tog, k12. Turn.

Row 9: Sl 1, k11, m1, p2 tog, k8.

Row 10: Cast off 5 sts, k2, p2 tog, k10. Turn.

Row 11: Sl 1, k9, m1, p2 tog, k1, m1, k2.

Row 12: K4, m1, p2 tog, k8. Turn.

Row 13: Sl 1, k7, m1, p2 tog, k2, m1, k2.

Row 14: K5, m1, p2 tog, k6. Turn.

Row 15: Sl 1, k5, m1, p2 tog, k3, m1, k2.

Row 16: K6, m1, p2 tog, k4. Turn.

Row 17: Sl 1, k3, m1, p2 tog, k2 tog, m2, k2, m1, k2.

Row 18: K6, p1, k1, m1, p2 tog, k2. Turn.

Row 19: Sl 1, k1, m1, p2 tog, k8.

Row 20: Cast off 5 sts, k2, m1, p2 tog, k2, (m1, k2 tog) 8 times, k2.

Repeat rows 1–20 until work forms circle.

Cast off.

To make up

Fix lavender sachet and half doll together, adding net underskirt following instructions on page 14.

Lightly press knitted circle. Thread fine yarn through holes at inner circle, adjust to fit the doll's waist. Decorate with silk ribbons as desired.

PERDITA

Materials

Lavender base 18 cm (7 inches) in diameter, made following instructions on page 13

1 × 20 g ball DMC 20 cotton

Pair needles 2 mm (14)

9 cm (3½ inch) half doll

Fine net for underskirt

Lavender and filling

Sewing cotton and needle

Narrow white ribbon to thread through holes at waist

Contrasting ribbon for bow at waist

Cast on 24 sts.

Row 1: Sl 1, k12, k2 tog, m1, k1, m1, k2 tog, k1, m1, k2 tog, m2, k2 tog, k1.

Row 2: K3, p1, k4, p14. Turn, leaving 3 sts on L.H. needle.

Row 3: K9, k2 tog, m1, k3, m1, k2 tog, k1, m1, k2 tog, m2, k2 tog, k1.

Row 4: K3, p1, k4, p15. Turn, leaving 3 sts on L.H. needle.

Row 5: K8, k2 tog, m1, k5, m1, k2 tog, k1, m1, k2 tog, m2, k2 tog, k1.

Row 6: K3, p1, k5, p15, k3.

Row 7: Sl 1, k2, p10, m1, sl 1, k1, psso, k1, k2 tog, m1, k4, m1, k2 tog, m2, k2 tog, k1.

Row 8: K3, p1, k7, p3, k11. Turn, leaving 3 sts on L.H. needle.

Row 9: P11, m1, sl 1, k2 tog, psso, m1, k6, m1, k2 tog, m2, k2 tog, k1.

Row 10: K3, p1, k22. Turn, leaving 3 sts on L.H. needle.

Row 11: P12, k14.

Row 12: Cast off 5 sts, k7, p1, k15.

Repeat rows 1–12 until length desired.

To make up

Fix lavender sachet and half doll together, adding underskirt of fine net as described on page 14.

Thread fine white ribbon through holes. Draw up lace to form circle. Place over lavender base.

28

Basket Cushion

Basket Cushion, a charming design by Ruth Rintoule based on patterns from an early knitting publication, features a wide edging with a coin-spot pattern and a garter stitch cushion centre with a knitted flower basket design. The incredible hand embroidered wholecloth homespun quilt, measuring 277 × 243 cm, is by Joan Jackson. Joan used DMC broder cotton in shades of cream and ecru to create this original design, an heirloom of the future. Titled 'Cream of the Crop', the quilt won the viewer's choice category in the members' exhibition presented by the Canberra Quilters Inc. Machine quilted. Courtesy Erina Walsh.

Materials

7 × 20 g balls DMC 10 cotton

Pair needles 2 mm (14)

Cotton fabric for cushion, 2 pieces 30 cm (12 in) square

50 cm silk ribbon

5 small buttons, 5 knitted flowers

Sewing thread and fine needle

Measurements

Centre square 23 cm (9 inches)

Coin-spot lace 9 cm (3½ inches) wide

Finished cushion 41 cm (16 inches) across

Knitted flowers 4 cm (1½ inches) across

Centre square

Cast on 107 sts. Knit 4 rows.

Row 1: ★K2, (m1, k2 tog). Repeat from ★ to last st, k1.

Row 2 and alternate Rows: Knit.

Repeat rows 1 and 2 three times.

Row 9: K2, (m1, k2 tog) 4 times, k to last 9 sts, (m1, k2 tog) 4 times, k1.

Row 10: Knit.

Repeat rows 9 and 10 until garter st forms a square.

Work rows 1 and 2 four times.

Knit 3 rows.

Cast off.

Coin-spot lace edging

Cast on 33 sts.

Row 1: Sl 1, k8, (m1, k2 tog) 3 times, k8, (k2 tog, m1) 3 times, k2, m1, k2.

Row 2: Knit.

Row 3: Sl 1, k2, (m1, k2 tog) 6 times, k8, (k2 tog, m1) 3 times, k3, m1, k2.

Row 4: Knit.

Row 5: Sl 1, k9, (m1, k2 tog) 3 times, k6, (k2 tog, m1) 4 times, k3, m1, k2.

Row 6: K28. Turn.

Row 7: K1, (m1, k2 tog) 4 times, k4, (k2 tog, m1) 5 times, k3, m1, k2.

Row 8: Knit.

Row 9: Sl 1, k8, (m1, k2) 8 times, k4, (k2 tog, m1) twice, k2, m1, k2.

Row 10: Knit.

Row 11: Sl 1, k3, (m1, k2 tog) 10 times, k6, (k2 tog, m1) twice, k2, m1, k2.

Row 12: Knit.

Row 13: Sl 1, k8, (m1, k2 tog) 7 times, k8, (k2 tog, m1) twice, k2, m1, k2.

Row 14: Knit 32. Turn.

Row 15: K1, (m1, k2 tog) 7 times, k8, (k2 tog, m1) twice, k2 tog, k1, m1, k2.

Row 16: Knit.

Row 17: Sl 1, k8, (m1, k2 tog) 7 times, k8, (k2 tog, m1) twice, k2 tog, k1, m1, k2.

Row 18: Knit 32. Turn.

Row 19: K1, (m1, k2 tog) 7 times, k8, (k2 tog, m1) twice, k2 tog, k1, m1, k2.

Row 20: K3, k2 tog, k35.

Row 21: Sl 1, k3, (m1, k2 tog) 10 times, k6, (k2 tog, m1) twice, k2 tog, k1, m1, k2.

Row 22: K3, k2 tog, k34.

Row 23: Sl 1, k8, (m1, k2 tog) 8 times, k4, (k2 tog, m1) twice, k2 tog, k1, m1, k2.

Row 24: K3, k2 tog, k33.

Row 25: Sl 1, k8, (m1, k2 tog) 4 times, k4, (k2 tog, m1) 5 times, k2 tog, k2, m1, k2.

Row 26: K3, k2 tog, k24. Turn.

Row 27: K2, (m1, k2 tog) 3 times, k6, (k2 tog, m1) 4 times, k2 tog, k2, m1, k2.

Row 28: K3, k2 tog, k31.

Row 29: Sl 1, k2, (m1, k2 tog) 6 times, k8, (k2 tog, m1) 3 times, k2 tog, k2, m1, k2.

Row 30: K3, k2 tog, k30.

Row 31: Sl 1, k8, (m1, k2 tog) 3 times, k8, (k2 tog, m1) 3 times, k2 tog, k1, m1, k2.

Row 32: K3, k2 tog, k29.

Repeat rows 1–32 until length required, allowing extra fullness at corners.

Basket motif

Cast on 33 sts.

Work rows 1–32 of Coin-spot lace edging twice.

Cast off.

Handle and basket edging

Cast on 5 sts.

Row 1: M1, (k2 tog) twice, k1.

Row 2: M1, knit to end of row.

Repeat these 2 rows until length required to edge basket motif and form handle.

Cast off.

Press the work. Join ends.

Flowers

(make 5)

Cast on 4 sts.

Row 1: (K1, m1) twice, k2.

Rows 2, 4 and 6: Knit.

Row 3: K2, m1, k2 tog, m1, k2.

Row 5: K3, m1, k2 tog, m1, k2.

Row 7: K4, m1, k2 tog, m1, k2.

Row 8: Cast off 5 sts. Knit to end.

Repeat rows 1–8 five times.

Cast off.

Press and join flower ends. Gather flower centre and attach to cushion. Sew button in centre.

Lace ribbon bows

(make 2)

Cast on 3 sts.

Row 1: M1, k2 tog, k1.

Repeat row 1 until length desired.

Cast off.

Press work and tie into bow.

To make up

Attach Coin-spot lace edging to centre square, allowing even fullness at corners. Pin basket motif in place, stitch to cushion centre. Join basket edging, stitch into position, then sew handle in place. Attach flowers as in the photograph. Tie both lace bows to basket handle. Thread narrow ribbon through holes at base of basket, using photograph for guidance.

Make a square cushion from the cotton fabric, leaving an opening to insert fibre filling and lavender. Close opening. Stitch lace top to cotton cushion.

29

Morwenna and the Dancers

(Pictured on page 78.) Morwenna, a Japanese half doll of fine porcelain, wears a wide lace skirt based on a nineteenth century pattern designed and knitted by the author. The two tiny porcelain figures at the front, also from the author's collection, wear skirts in the Helston pattern knitted by the author.

MORWENNA

Materials

Lavender base 18 cm (7 inches) in diameter, made in fine lavender cotton following instructions on page 13

2 × 20 g balls DMC 100 cotton, blanc

20 g DMC 12 cotton for narrow lace

2 pairs needles, 1.25 mm (18) and 1.00 mm (20)

9 cm (3½ inch) half doll

Pearl to fasten lace

Narrow ribbon

Sewing cotton to knit rose

Lavender and soft filling

Sewing thread and fine needle

Using 1.25 mm (18) needles:

Cast on 53 sts.

Row 1: Sl 1, k1, k2 tog, m2, k2 tog, k5, k2 tog, m2, (k2 tog) twice, m2, k2 tog, k8, k2 tog, m2, (k2 tog) twice, m2, k2 tog, k5, k2 tog, m2, k2 tog, k2, k2 tog, m2, k2 tog, k3.

Row 2: (K5, p1) twice, k8, p1, k3, p1, k11, p1, k3, p1, k8, p1, k3.

Row 3: Sl 1, k3, k2 tog, m2, k2 tog, k5, k2 tog, m2, k2 tog, k12, k2 tog, m2, k2 tog, k5, k2 tog, m2, k2 tog, k6, k2 tog, m2, k2, inc in last st.

Row 4: K5, p1, k9, p1, k8, p1, k15, p1, k8, p1, k5.

Row 5: Sl 1, k1, k2 tog, m2, (k2 tog) twice, m2, k2 tog, k5, k2 tog, m2, k2 tog, k8, k2 tog, m2, k2 tog, k5, k2 tog, m2, k2 tog, k10, k2 tog, m2, k2, inc in last st.

Row 6: K5, p1, k13, p1, k8, p1, k11, p1, k8, (p1, k3) twice.

Row 7: Sl 1, k3, k2 tog, m2, (k2 tog) twice, m2, k2 tog, k5, k2 tog, m2, k2 tog, k4, k2 tog, m2, k2 tog, k5, k2 tog, m2, k2 tog, k14, k2 tog, m2, k2, inc in last st.

Row 8: K5, p1, k17, p1, k8, p1, k7, p1, k8, p1, k3, p1, k5.

Row 9: Sl 1, k1, k2 tog, m2, (k2 tog) twice, m2, (k2 tog) twice, m2, k2 tog, k5, k2 tog, m2, (k2 tog) twice, m2, k2 tog, k5, k2 tog, m2, k2 tog, k18, k2 tog, m2, k2, inc in last st.

Row 10: K5, p1, k21, p1, k8, p1, k3, p1, k8, (p1, k3) 3 times.

Row 11: Sl 1, k3, k2 tog, m2, (k2 tog) twice, m2, (k2 tog) twice, m2, k2 tog, k5, k2 tog, m2, k2 tog, k5, k2 tog, m2, k2 tog, k22, k2 tog, m2, k3.

Row 12: K4, p1, k25, (p1, k8) twice, (p1, k3) twice, p1, k5.

Row 13: Sl 1, k1, k2 tog, m2, (k2 tog) twice, m2, (k2 tog) twice, m2, k2 tog, k5, k2 tog, m2, (k2 tog) twice, m2, k2 tog, k5, k2 tog, m2, k2 tog, k18, k2 tog, m2, (k2 tog) 3 times.

Row 14: K2 tog, k2, p1, k21, p1, k8, p1, k3, p1, k8, (p1, k3) 3 times.

Row 15: Sl 1, k3, k2 tog, m2, (k2 tog) twice, m2, k2 tog, k5, k2 tog, m2, k2 tog, k4, k2 tog, m2, k2 tog, k5, k2 tog, m2, k2 tog, k14, k2 tog, m2, (k2 tog) twice, k1.

Row 16: K2 tog, k2, p1, k17, p1, k8, p1, k7, p1, k8, p1, k3, p1, k5.

Row 17: Sl 1, k1, k2 tog, m2, (k2 tog) twice, m2, k2 tog, k5, k2 tog, m2, k2 tog, k8, k2 tog, m2, k2 tog, k5, k2 tog, m2, k2 tog, k10, k2 tog, m2, (k2 tog) twice, k1.

Row 18: K2 tog, k2, p1, k13, p1, k8, p1, k11, p1, k8, (p1, k3) twice.

Row 19: Sl 1, k3, k2 tog, m2, k2 tog, k5, k2 tog, m2, k2 tog, k12, k2 tog, m2, k2 tog, k5, k2 tog, m2, k2 tog, k6, k2 tog, m2, (k2 tog) twice, k1.

Row 20: K2 tog, k2, p1, k9, p1, k8, p1, k15, p1, k8, p1, k5.

Repeat rows 1–20 until length desired, ending work on row 2.

To make up

Fix lavender sachet and half doll together.

Press the lace. Thread a length of fine ribbon through holes at top. Gently gather to form circle. Adjust to fit doll's waist, tie at back in a double bow. Stitch knitted rose at waist in front.

The doll in the photograph has been given a length of woven braid as a 'bodice'.

Lace collar

Using DMC 12 and 1.25 (18) needles, cast on 4 sts.

Row 1: Sl 1, k1, m1, k2.

Row 2: K5.

Row 3: Sl 1, k2, m1, k2.

Row 4: K6.

Row 5: Sl 1, k1, m2, k2 tog, m1, k2.

Row 6: K5, p1, k2.

Row 7: Sl 1, k5, m1, k2.

Row 8: Cast off 5 sts, k3.

Repeat rows 1–8 until lace is length required to edge neckline.

Cast off.

Lightly press, attach with a small pearl if desired.

Sewing-cotton rose

Using fine sewing cotton and 1.00 mm (20) needles:

Cast on 10 sts.

Row 1: K1, (m1, k1) to end of row.

Repeat row 1 twice.

Cast off and form into flower with your fingers. Sew to ribbon sash at waistline.

(Use two shades of cotton together, one strand of each, for a larger rose like the one illustrated.)

HELSTON DANCERS

Two dancing porcelain figures, named after the Cornish Floral Dance held at Helston in Cornwall each year on 8 May, with knitted lace overskirts and lavender sachets tucked underneath. From the author's collection.

Materials

1 × 50 g ball DMC 20 cotton

Pair needles 1.75 mm (16)

13 cm (5½ inch) figurine

Ribbon for waist

Small piece lawn

Lavender

Sewing cotton and needle

Cast on 24 sts.

Row 1: Sl 1, k20, m1, k2 tog, k1.

Row 2: M1, k2 tog, k7, p10. Turn.

Row 3: Sl 1, k14, m1, k2 tog, m1, k2.

Row 4: M1, k2 tog, k8, p10. Turn.

Row 5: Sl 1, k13, (m1, k2 tog) twice, m1, k2.

Row 6: M1, k2 tog, k9, p10, m1, k2 tog, k3.

Row 7: Sl 1, 4, p10, k3, (m1, k2 tog) 3 times, m1, k2.

Row 8: M1, k2 tog, k20. Turn.

Row 9: Sl 1, p9, k2, (m1, k2 tog) 4 times, m1, k2.

Row 10: M1, k2 tog, k21. Turn.

Row 11: Sl 1, p9, k1, (m1, k2 tog) 5 times, m1, k2.

Row 12: M1, k2 tog, k12, p10, m1, k2 tog, k3.

Row 13: Sl 1, k15, k2 tog, (m1, k2 tog) 5 times, k1.

Row 14: M1, k2 tog, k11, p10. Turn.

Row 15: Sl 1, k11, k2 tog, (m1, k2 tog) 4 times, k1.

Row 16: M1, k2 tog, k10, p10. Turn.

Row 17: Sl 1, k12, k2 tog, (m1, k2 tog) 3 times, k1.

Row 18: M1, k2 tog, k19, m1, k2 tog, k3

Row 19: Sl 1, k4, p10, k4, k2 tog, (m1, k2 tog) twice, k1.

Row 20: M1, k2 tog, k18. Turn.

Row 21: Sl 1, p9, k5, k2 tog, m1, k2 tog, k1.

Row 22: M1, k2 tog, k17. Turn.

Row 23: Sl 1, p9, k9.

Row 24: M1, k2 tog, k17, m1, k2 tog, k3.

Repeat rows 1–24 until length desired.

Cast off.

To make up

Make a small strip lavender sachet to help hold out the skirt, and act as a petticoat.

Thread ribbon through holes at top edge of knitted lace skirt. Tie around waist with bow at back, leaving long tails to the hemline. Place lavender sachet under skirt.

30

Reseda

Master knitter Ruth Rintoule created this delightful embroidered sachet 15 cm (6 inches) square from a small sample of furnishing fabric, edged with an incredible example of her knitting.

Materials

1 × 20 g ball DMC 60 cotton

Pair needles 1.25 mm (18)

Piece of firm green fabric 9 cm (3½ inches) square for sachet front

DMC stranded cottons:

–800 Blue for French knots

–3078 Lemon

Silk ribbons:

–128 Rose for wound rose

–8 Pink for detached chain

–33 Green for ribbon stitch

Needle and thread

Length of narrow ribbon to thread through beading

Button

Lace edging and beading are 4 cm (1½ inches) wide

Cast on 16 sts.

Row 1: Sl 1, k5, (m1, k2 tog) twice, m3, k2 tog, k1, m1, k2 tog, m1, k1.

Row 2: K6, p1, k1, p1, k10.

Row 3: Sl 1, k6, (m1, k2 tog) twice, k4, k2 tog, m1, k2.

Row 4 and alternate Rows: Knit.

Row 5: Sl 1, k7, (m1, k2 tog) twice, k3, k2 tog, m1, k2.

Row 7: Sl 1, k8, (m1, k2 tog) twice, k2, k2 tog, m1, k2.

Row 9: Sl 1, k9, (m1, k2 tog) twice, k1, k2 tog, m1, k2.

Row 11: Sl 1, k10, (m1, k2 tog) twice, k2 tog, m1, k2.

Row 13: Sl 1, k11, (m1, k2 tog) twice, k3.

Row 14: Cast off 3 sts, k to end of row.

Repeat rows 1–14 until length desired.

Beading

Cast on 5 sts.

Row 1: M1, p2 tog, k1, m1, k2.

Row 2: K2, (k1, p1, k1) into m1 of previous row, k1, m1, p2 tog.

Row 3: M1, p2 tog, k6.

Row 4: K6, m1, p2 tog.

Row 5: M1, p2 tog, k6.

Row 6: Cast off 3 sts. K2, m1, p2 tog.

Repeat rows 1–6 until length desired.

Cast off.

To make up

Make sachet 7 cm (2¾ inches) square following instructions on page 13. Stitch lace edging around embroidered centre, adjusting lace around corners. Press knitted beading, and sew to lace edging with points facing centre of sachet. Thread narrow green ribbon through beading, tie bow in one corner.

Make a loop at back of sachet. Sew on button to close.

31

Red Rose

A linen sachet 18 cm (7 inches) square, embroidered by Joan Jackson and edged with a fine lace from an 1897 design knitted by the author.

Materials

2 pieces of fine linen 20 cm (8 inches) square

DMC embroidery threads 326, 349, 3347, 727, 776

1 × 20 g ball DMC 12 cotton

Pair needles 1.25 mm (18)

Lavender

Fibre filling

Sewing and embroidery needles

Sewing thread

Fine ribbon (optional)

Cast on 7 sts.

Row 1: Sl 1, (m1, k2 tog) 3 times.

Row 2: M1, k1, p4, k2.

Row 3: Sl 1, k1, (m1, k2 tog) 3 times.

Row 4: M1, k1, p4, k3.

Row 5: Sl 1, k2, (m1, k2 tog) 3 times.

Row 6: M1, k1, p4, k4.

Row 7: Sl 1, k3, (m1, k2 tog) 3 times.

Row 8: M1, k1, p4, k3. Turn.

Row 9: Sl 1, k2, (m1, k2 tog) 3 times.

Row 10: K2, p4, k5.

Row 11: Sl 1, k2, k2 tog, (m1, k2 tog) 3 times.

Row 12: K2, p4, k4.

Row 13: (K2 tog) twice, (m1, k2 tog) 3 times.

Row 14: K2, p4, k2.

Row 15: K2 tog, (m1, k2 tog) 3 times.

Row 16: K2, p4, k1.

Repeat rows 1–16 until length desired.

Cast off.

To make up

Joan embroidered the front of the sachet in a freeform design, using 1 strand only for the smaller flowers. Make up sachet following instructions on page 13.

Press the lace and attach to sachet with fine stitches, easing around the corners. You may wish to add a ribbon bow to one corner.

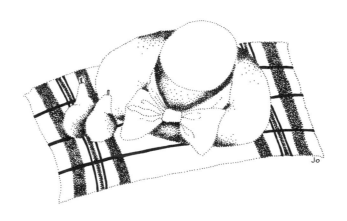

32

Alexia

Two versions of a popular nineteenth century lace edging knitted by the author.

CUFFS

Materials

1 × 20 g ball DMC 20 cotton

Pair needles 2 mm (14)

Make 2.

Cast on 15 sts. Knit one row.

Row 1: K2, m4 (k2 tog, m1) 5 times, k2 tog, k1.

Row 2: K12, (k1, p1) twice, k2.

Rows 3 and 4: K18.

Row 5: K2, m5, k2 tog, k1, (m1, k2 tog) 6 times, k1.

Row 6: K15, (k1, p1) twice, k3.

Rows 7 and 8: K22.

Row 9: Cast off 7 sts, k1, m4, (k2 tog, m1) 5 times, k2 tog, k1.

Repeat rows 2–9 eleven times or to length required.

To make up

Press the cuffs, spray with starch and press again under a dry cloth. Use cuff links or a decorative button closure.

BLACK LACE

Materials

1 × 20 g ball DMC 80 cotton, noir

Pair needles 1 mm (20)

Cast on 17 sts.

Row 1: Sl 1, k3, (m1, k2 tog) 5 times. Cast on 4 sts, k2 tog, k1.

Row 2: K20.

Row 3: Sl 1, k13, (k1, p1) in each of next 4 sts, k2.

Row 4: K24

Row 5: Sl 1, k3, (m1, k2 tog) 5 times, k10.

Rows 6 and 7: Knit.

Row 8: Cast off 7 sts, k16.

Repeat rows 1–8 until length desired.

33

Spanish Point Lace

A small sleep sachet measuring 23 cm × 27 cm (9 × 10½ inches). Ideal to use under the pillow to perfume the bed. The sachet, designed and made by the author, has a mesh centre edged with the popular nineteenth century Spanish Point lace.

Materials

1 × 50 g ball DMC 10 cotton

Pair needles 2 mm (14)

1 × 10 g ball DMC 12 cotton for rosettes

Pair double-pointed needles 1.75 mm (16)

Basic lavender-filled cushion to fit

4 buttons

Needle and thread

Filet mesh centre

Cast on 40 sts.

Row 1: ★K4, m2. Repeat from ★ to last 4 sts, k4.

Row 2: K2, ★ k2 tog, (k1, p1) in m2 of previous row, k2 tog. Repeat from ★ to last 4 sts, k2 tog, k2.

Row 3: K2, m1, ★ k4, m2. Repeat from ★ to last 6 sts, k4, m1, k2.

Row 4: K3, k2 tog, ★ k2 tog, (k1, p1) in m2 of previous row, k2 tog. Repeat from ★ to last 5 sts, k2 tog, k3.

Repeat rows 1–4 until work measures 15 cm (6 inches). Cast off.

Spanish Point lace edging

Special instruction

In the row following the m3 instruction work k1, p1, k1 in the made sts.

Cast on 19 sts.

Row 1: Sl 1, k2, m1, k2 tog, k2, m1, sl 1, k1, psso, k3, k2 tog, m1, k3, m1, k2.

Row 2: M1, k2 tog, k15, m1, k2 tog, k1.

Row 3: Sl 1, k2, m1, k2 tog, k3, m1, sl 1, k1, psso, k1, k2 tog, m1, k5, m1, k2.

Row 4: M1, k2 tog, k16, m1, k2 tog, k1.

Row 5: Sl 1, k2, m1, k2 tog, k4, m1, sl 1, k2 tog, psso, m1, sl 1, k1, psso, k2 tog, m3, k2 tog, k1, m1, k2.

Row 6: M1, k2 tog, k4, (k1, p1, k1) in m3 of previous row, p1, k12, m1, k2 tog, k1.

Row 7: Sl 1, k2, m1, k2 tog, k2, k2 tog, m1, k3, m1, sl 1, k1, psso, k3, k2 tog, m1, k2 tog, k1.

Row 8: M1, k2 tog, k16, m1, k2 tog, k1.

Row 9: Sl 1, k2, m1, k2 tog, k1, k2 tog, m1, k5, m1, sl 1, k1, psso, k1, k2 tog, m1, k2 tog, k1.

Row 10: M1, k2 tog, k15, m1, k2 tog, k1.

Row 11: Sl 1, k2, m1, (k2 tog) twice, m1, sl 1, k1, psso, k2 tog, m3, k2 tog, k1, m1, sl 1, k2 tog, psso, m1, k2 tog, k1.

Row 12: M1, k2 tog, k6, (k1, p1, k1) in m3 of previous row, p1, k7, m1, k2 tog, k1.

Repeat rows 1–12 until length required, allowing for fullness around the corners.

Rosette cord

Worked in DMC 12 cotton on 1.75 mm (16) double-pointed needles thus:

Cast on 3 sts.

Row 1: ★K3. Do not turn. Slide sts to other end of needle. Pull yarn firmly★. Repeat from ★—★ to make length required to shape into a rosette like those in the photograph. End off by k3 tog, and darning in end, or sl 1, k2 tog, psso, fasten off.

Make another three rosettes.

To make up

Make basic lavender-filled sachet following the instructions on page 13.

Press knitted work under damp cloth. Stitch Spanish Point lace around the sachet centre, allowing sufficient fullness at each corner. Stitch ends of lace together. Sew a small button at each corner of the lavender-filled sachet and button the lace cover into position. Stitch a fine cord rosette in each corner to conceal the buttons.

Bibliography

Abbey, Barbara *Knitting Lace*, Schoolhouse Press, Pittsville, Wisconsin, reprinted 1993.

De Dillmont, Thérèse, *Encyclopedia of Needlework*, DMC Publications, Mulhouse, France 1924, 2nd ed 1978.

Fancy and Practical Knitting, The Butterick Publishing Co, London and New York, 1897.

Klickman, Flora *The Modern Knitting Book*, published by The Girls' Own and Woman's Magazine, London 1914.

Lewis, Susanna E. *Knitting Lace*, Taunton Press, USA, 1992.

Mrs Leach's Fancy Work Basket, R. S. Cartwright, London, 1887.

Needlecraft Practical Journals, W. Briggs & Co. Ltd, Manchester 1911, 1930.

Rutt, The Rt Rev. Richard *A History of Hand Knitting*, B. T. Batsford Ltd, London, 1987.

Sibbald and Souter, *Dainty Work for Busy Fingers*, S. W. Partridge & Co. Ltd, London, 1915.

Thomas, Mary *Mary Thomas's Book of Knitting Patterns*, Hodder & Stoughton Ltd, London, 1985.

Weldon's Practical Knitter, series published by Weldon Ltd, The Strand, London, c.1890–1911.

Wright, Mary *Cornish Guernseys and Knit Frocks*, Alison Hodges, Cornwall, 1979.

Wright Mary *Granny's Lace Knitting and Great Granny's Lace Knitting*, self published, Cornwall, 1986.

Zimmerman, Elizabeth *Knitter's Almanac*, Dover, New York, 1981.

Zimmerman, Elizabeth *Knitting Around*, Schoolhouse Press, Pittsville, Wisconsin, 1989.

Suppliers

DMC Needlecraft Pty Ltd
51–55 Carrington Road
Marrickville NSW 2204
(02) 9559 3088

Queanbeyan Book and Prints
Millhouse Gallery
49 Collett Street
Queanbeyan NSW 2620
(02) 6297 3067

Fyshwick Antique Centre
72 Kembla Street
Fyshwick ACT 2609
(02) 6280 4541

Macleod Gallery
Shop 7, Albion Centre
Wallace Street
Braidwood NSW 2622
(02) 4842 2626
Lavender flowers

Tinkers Antiques
23 Sydney Road
Mogo NSW 2536
(02) 4474 4834
Half dolls

Pat Blyth
Reproduction half dolls
Mobile 0414 845 981 only
Canberra ACT

Ria Wark
Dollworks
Narrabundah Shops
45 Boolimba Crescent
Narrabundah ACT 2604
(02) 6295 0697

Oakey Creek Lavender Farm
Colin Bates (Prop)
via Hall, ACT 2618
(02) 6230 2140

Crisp-Gro Lavender Nursery
Gap Range
Bowning NSW 2582
(02) 6227 6032

Index

Other books by Furze Hewitt

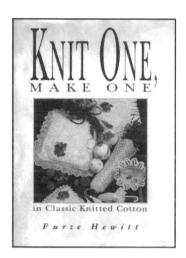

Knit One, Make One in Classic Knitted Cotton

This book illustrates the full potential of knitted textiles and the delicate beauty of white cotton knitting. The collection of one hundred patterns includes easy-to-follow patterns for soft furnishings and gift ideas of all kinds to suit traditional and modern decors. Knitting novices will find items that they can tackle with ease, while knitting experts will be able to exercise their abilities with the larger, more complex pieces.

How you use the designs depends on you. By changing the application of the designs you will add your personal touch, and provide your family with an heirloom of your creation.

Motifs, Borders and Trims in Classic Knitted Cotton

The motifs, borders and trims in this book can be joined together to make articles of any size. Traditionally these nineteenth century motifs were used to make white knitted cotton bedspreads, but knitters who are less ambitious may prefer to make cot covers, shawls or even doll's wraps. The possibilities for soft furnishings and decorator items are limitless – cushion covers, blinds, wall hangings, lamp shades... The borders can be used as attractive edgings for larger items, and the trims to finish off smaller or more delicate articles. There are simple yet effective patterns for beginners, and patterns which get progressively more challenging for experienced knitters.

Traditional Lace Knitting

This collection of forty projects to knit for pleasure in fine cotton ranges from generous lace edgings for full length calico curtains to table toppers, a tray cloth, tea cloths and napkins, preserve covers, coat hangers, baby blankets, two dolls' dresses, Nicholas Spruce the green Christmas bear (and other Christmas items), edgings for a twelve-place banquet cloth, towels, sheets and pillowcases, a pomander, a sleep sachet and a decorative rosette.

The patterns, some written over a century ago, have been reworded in modern English and adapted where necessary while retaining their timeless charm.

This is a book to tempt and inspire all lovers of fine knitting.

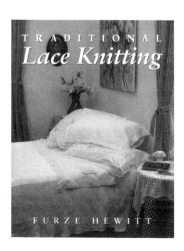